50 YEARS OF THE RED ARROWS

50 YEARS OF THE RED ARROWS

PETER R. MARCH

The History Press

First published 2014
Reprinted 2014, 2015, 2016

The History Press
The Mill, Brimscombe Port
Stroud, Gloucestershire, GL5 2QG
www.thehistorypress.co.uk

British Library Cataloguing in Publication Data.
A catalogue record for this book is available from the British Library.

ISBN 978 0 7509 5634 5

Typesetting and origination by The History Press
Printed in India by Replika Press Pvt. Ltd.

CONTENTS

ACKNOWLEDGEMENTS

The story of the Royal Air Force Aerobatic Team, the *Red Arrows*, across five decades since the team was formed as part of the Central Flying School in 1965 is fascinating. The more you look into it the more interesting it becomes. What is rather difficult though is to produce a truly representative account in words and pictures of those busy years. I am therefore very grateful to several colleagues for allowing me to include some of their words and photographs. In particular Jamie Hunter's description of a flight with the *Red Arrows* in April 2006, the fascinating account of the team's *Springhawk* pre-season training at RAF Akrotiri, Cyprus, interviews with individual team members and an outstanding collection of air-to-air photographs give added life to this review.

Aviation journalist Ben Dunnell has generously contributed extracts from recent interviews with two former *Red Arrows* pilots that give unique insights into the team's formative years and the transition from the Gnat to the Hawk. Glen Moreman has also provided an account of the team's 'Kemble Years' and contemporary photographs for use in this book. Selecting a relatively small number from the huge stock of *Red Arrows* Hawk photographs available to me was a nice problem to have. I would like to thank Andrew and Daniel March, Adrian Balch, Brian Strickland, Denis Calvert, Katsuhiko Tokunaga, Kevin Storer, Lindsay Peacock, Paul Fiddian, Pete Mobbs and BAE Systems for providing so many outstanding images that capture both the routine and the more significant moments across the *Red Arrows*' years.

I am indebted to Paul Fiddian for his helpful research, additions to the text and overall review of the book. Brian Strickland has managed the photo sourcing and scanning with great care. I am grateful to former *Red Arrows* manager Andy Stewart and public relations officer Tony Cunnane for permission to use material they originally produced for the Royal Air Force Yearbook.

I would like to dedicate this celebratory book to the memory of the late Ray Hanna. There is no doubt that it was his skilled leadership from 1966 to 1969 that set the team on its incredible path to worldwide acclaim. Ray epitomised the excellence of the *Red Arrows* throughout his forty years of air-show flying, initially while serving with the RAF and subsequently displaying Spitfire IX MH434 and other warbirds.

PETER R. MARCH

I was closely connected with the *Red Arrows* when we were flying from Fairford and they were at Kemble, a short distance away, in the early 1970s. In fact, I was in the pre-production Concorde 01 when it flew in formation with the *Red Arrows* and vividly remember that occasion. In those days they flew the Gnat.

I was privileged to have a flight in the leader's Gnat for a formation practice. I was fascinated by it. I expected the whole thing would be too much for me but I was impressed by the smoothness with which everything was done. This was all down to the leader's skill and the ability of the other team members to follow accordingly. These pilots are very highly trained and very talented, but above all they are an immense national asset.

They bring great credit on this country, and we should remember that when we hear talk of defence cuts and wonder if the *Red Arrows* are going to fall victim. That should never happen. They are a great national institution and I wish them many more years of flying.

THE LATE BRIAN TRUBSHAW,
CHIEF TEST PILOT OF CONCORDE

△ Brian Trubshaw flying the pre-production Concorde G-AXDN led by the *Red Arrows'* scarlet-painted Gnats. (Arthur Gibson Collection)

◁ Squadron Leader Ray Hanna, longest-serving leader of the *Red Arrows*, flying Spitfire IX MH434 as *Red 1* at the Royal International Air Tattoo in July 1996, marking the sixtieth anniversary of the Spitfire's first flight. (Daniel J. March)

INTRODUCTION

You would be hard-pressed to find someone in the UK who has not heard of or seen the Royal Air Force's *Red Arrows*, such is the team's reach and presence. The aerial spectacle that they create can only draw admiration. They can make a crowd gasp, flinch and wholeheartedly applaud. The team prides itself on its absolute precision – the product of intense hard work, professionalism and dedication. Each of the nine pilots is very aware of the equally dedicated support team that fulfils a diversity of tasks to ensure that the show goes on throughout the summer months.

The team is one of Britain's great international ambassadors and the showpiece of the Royal Air Force, displaying their skills and airmanship in a tradition that goes back to the 1920s. The *Red Arrows* are universally acknowledged wherever they perform, both for their brilliant displays and the qualities of the aircraft they fly, the BAe Hawk advanced jet trainer. Very much the public face of the Royal Air Force, the team enhances the services' reputation on many fronts and has been of considerable benefit to British trade and industry. On overseas visits BAE Systems, which manufactures the latest version of the Hawk, has been able to build on the team's high profile to encourage an interest in the aircraft by air arms in many countries. This has helped to secure multimillion-pound contracts for the company, engine manufacturer Rolls-Royce and a host of other aviation companies around the UK.

Up to the end of 2013, the *Red Arrows* had given 4,562 displays in fifty-five different countries from Australia and Zimbabwe to Bangladesh and Ukraine. The appreciative crowds have ranged from just a few hundred at Goose Bay to a staggering 650,000 in Portugal in June 1973 and nearly one million along Sydney waterfront in 1996.

▷ The *Red Arrows* flew bright red-painted Gnats from 1965 to 1979.

The team's nine-aircraft close-formation routines and breathtaking sequences by the *Synchro* performers have been the subject of many hours of colourful television programmes, beamed across the world and watched by countless viewers.

Formally established on 1 March 1965, the team was initially based at RAF Fairford, Gloucestershire, which was then a satellite of the RAF's Central Flying School (CFS). It comprised seven display pilots (plus a reserve) flying red-painted Folland/Hawker Siddeley Gnat advanced training aircraft.

In its first full year, the *Red Arrows* gave sixty-five displays in Britain, France, Italy, Holland, Belgium and Germany. In 1968, the team was extended to fly nine Gnats. Since then the signature 'Diamond Nine' formation has come to represent the peak of precision flying and is now the team's globally recognised trademark.

Aerobatics has played a prominent part in the RAF since its inception as the world's first independent air force back in 1918. In pilot training it allows a new pilot to develop confidence in himself and his aircraft. Formation flying is an essential part of the tactical operations of any front-line squadron, and formation aerobatics not only encourages the growth of confidence in a leader and other members of the formation but also develops team spirit.

The team took delivery of Hawk T1 jet trainers in late 1979, the pilots converting from Gnats and working up using the new aircraft in time for the 1980 summer display season.

The Royal Air Force Aerobatic Team, the *Red Arrows*, continues today as an important RAF Unit whose primary role is to demonstrate the teamwork and excellence of performance demanded of all RAF personnel.

The *Red Arrows* stand alone. They are appreciated and have achieved the basic essential in aerobatic demonstration, which is unbroken continuity of manoeuvre from take-off to landing.

GROUP CAPTAIN SIR DOUGLAS BADER

▷ Hawks replaced the Gnats in 1979 and still equip the team today.

All photographs Peter R. March/PRM Aviation Collection unless otherwise credited.

△ *Black Arrows* Hunters of 'Treble-One' Squadron.

1 THE BEGINNING

It is becoming hard to recall a time when the *Red Arrows* was not the RAF's premier display team. In fact you have to go back to 1964 and the Central Flying School's *Red Pelicans* to find the *Arrows*' predecessor. The last official RAF aerobatic team to fly front-line fighter aircraft was No. 56 Squadron's *Firebirds* team, with nine red- and silver-painted English Electric Lightnings, in 1963.

Without doubt the most famous operational aircraft to be flown by the RAF's premier team was the Hawker Hunter. In 1957, No. 111 Squadron's team of five black-painted Hunters became known as the *Black Arrows*. At the following year's SBAC Show at Farnborough 'Treble One' Squadron provided the spectacle of a twenty-two Hunter loop, the greatest number of aircraft ever looped in formation. The *Black Arrows* continued as the RAF's aerobatic team until 1961, when it was replaced by the *Blue Diamonds* of No. 92 Squadron.

Lightnings of No. 74 Squadron, the *Tigers*, were given the leading role in 1962 and No. 56 Squadron, the *Firebirds*, took the mantle in 1963. It was decided in that year, for operational and economic reasons, that the RAF's leading team should be drawn from a training unit, rather than from front-line fighter squadrons. So, in 1964, the *Red Pelicans*, flying six Jet Provost T4s from RAF Little Rissington, Gloucestershire, became the first Central Flying School team since the early 1930s to be given the accolade. Despite an extremely polished aerobatic display, the relatively slow and ungainly Jet Provost compared unfavourably with the sleek Hunter and powerful Lightning, reducing the impact of the team's performance.

▽ Representing RAF teams past and present, a *Yellowjacks*-painted Gnat followed by *Black Arrows* and *Blue Diamonds* Hunters with the *Red Arrows*' Hawks for a flypast at Biggin Hill, September 2005.

▷ *Yellowjacks* Gnats flying with the 1964 RAF Aerobatic Team, the *Red Pelicans*.

▽ Twenty-two Hunters of 'Treble One' Squadron *Black Arrows* looping at Farnborough in 1958.

▷ The *Blue Diamonds* of No. 92 Squadron with sixteen Hunters practicing in June 1961.

▽ Colourful *Firebirds* Lightning T4 and F1As lined up at RAF Wattisham at the start of the 1963 season.

◁ The official RAF Aerobatic
Team in 1964 was the
CFS *Red Pelicans* with
red-painted Jet Provost T4s.

2 YELLOWJACKS

In 1964, an aerobatic team was formed at No. 4 Flying Training School at RAF Valley to see if the Gnat T1 could effectively be used as a display aircraft. Five yellow painted Gnats, flown by instructors from 4FTS under Flight Lieutenant Lee Jones' leadership, displayed as the *Yellowjacks*.

While Lee Jones was well qualified to lead the Gnat team, having previously been a member of the *Black Arrows*, the famous Hunter team, there was some uncertainty about the aircraft. The Gnat had only entered service in 1962 and still had a number of introductory problems. The Aeroplane and Armament Experimental Establishment at Boscombe Down had warned, in a handling assessment, that it might not prove very practicable for formation aerobatics.

However, the team found they could put on a good show and were able to overcome the initially unimpressive nature of the Gnat, which lacked the fantastic noise and visible fires of the supersonic types on full reheat. This was achieved by sheer grace, precision and an extended repertoire of slick formation changes.

▽ Yellow-painted Gnats of the aptly named *Yellowjacks* team performed at Farnborough in September 1964. (Adrian Balch)

The *Yellowjacks* were allocated ten aircraft (XR540, XR901-6, XR986-7 and XS111) for their five-ship display routine. As it turned out, this was an unnecessarily generous provision.

The swept-wing Gnat was an ideal compromise between the front-line jet fighters and the less attractive basic jet trainers, as the team's symmetrical formation shapes brought back the sleek appearance that the public had grown accustomed to in the displays of earlier years.

The *Yellowjacks* gave their first public display at the RNAS Culdrose Air Day on 25 July 1964 and were an instant success. This was underlined by their reception after appearing at the Farnborough Air Show in September, which influenced the decision to establish the new Gnat team as part of the Central Flying School (CFS) at RAF Little Rissington. The team was to be run on the lines of a normal RAF squadron, but dedicated wholly to aerobatic flying at air displays and on other occasions.

▽ The *Yellowjacks* preparing to taxi at RAF Little Rissington in August 1964.

However, one major problem had to be overcome. The team had been named the *Yellowjacks* because of the yellow-painted Gnats they flew, but the then commandant of the Central Flying School, Air Commodore Bird-Wilson, apparently hated the title and insisted on a name change.

Lee Jones, who had no fear of senior officers, appeared to acquiesce to authority and for a short time the team was known by the preposterous name *Daffodils*. The Gnats were then painted red, probably to ensure that the name

Yellowjacks (or *Daffodils*) could no longer be used. When asked to suggest a name for the new team to Bird-Wilson, Lee said: 'Let it be *Red Arrows* – *Red* for the colour, and *Arrows* in memory of the *Black Arrows*.'

3 RED ARROWS

Like the *Red Pelicans* before it, the new team was established on an annual basis as part of the CFS at RAF Little Rissington, Gloucestershire. It was officially dubbed the *Red Arrows*, adopting the colour associated with the CFS and the arrow-like shape of the Gnat and its formations from the earlier 'Treble One' Squadron Hunter team. The ten red-painted Gnats were initially based at RAF Fairford as a CFS detachment.

The *Red Arrows* first displayed for the press at RAF Little Rissington on 6 May 1965 and made their public debut in the UK at the Biggin Hill Air Fair nine days later. This was followed by over sixty appearances that year, including visits to Belgium, France, Italy, the Netherlands and West Germany. As Air Fair organiser the late Jock Maitland recalled, 'Right from the start, the *Red Arrows*' display was of a very, very high standard. Today, the presentation

▷ 'Seven Arrow Roll' at the RAF Little Rissington press display on 8 May 1965.

▷ 'Vixen Break' by the *Red Arrows* at their first UK public display at Biggin Hill on 15 May 1965.

◁ Flight Lieutenant Lee Jones (left) briefing the team before the *Red Arrows'* first display for the press at RAF Little Rissington in 1965.

is perhaps a little bit more slick, but the 1965 team put on a very fine show indeed.' *Flight* magazine agreed, its reporter commenting in particular on 'the team's downward bomb-burst with smoke, on which two aircraft then superimposed an upward burst'.

A few weeks later they formed part of the RAF's presentation at the Paris Air Show at Le Bourget, this time in concert with Lightning F3s of No. 111 Squadron. Not even the commentator's rather incongruous choice of 'Roll out the Barrel' as the accompaniment could dampen the enthusiasm of the French public for the RAF's skills. At the end of 1965 the *Arrows* were awarded the Britannia Trophy by the Royal Aero Club in recognition of their outstanding contribution to British prestige in the field of aviation.

In 1966 the seven-aircraft team was under the leadership of newly promoted Squadron Leader Ray Hanna, and just under ninety shows were flown by the end of the season. Technical problems with the Gnat, which meant a detailed structural check of each aircraft was needed, delayed the start of the 1967 season. But nevertheless nearly 100 public appearances were made that year.

◁ The 1966 team, with Squadron Leader Ray Hanna at its forefront. With him are Flight Lieutenant Derek Bell (*Red 2*), Flight Lieutenant Bill Langworthy (*Red 3*), Flight Lieutenant Peter Evans (*Red 4*), Flight Lieutenant Roy Booth (*Red 5*), Flight Lieutenant Henry Prince (*Red 6*), Flight Lieutenant Timothy Nelson (*Red 7*), Flight Lieutenant Frank Hoare (*Red 8*) and Flight Lieutenant Douglas McGregor (*Red 9*).

4 KEMBLE YEARS

Although the RAF Central Flying School (CFS) was officially based at RAF Little Rissington, because of the Gnat's higher speed and the rather crowded airfield circuit the *Red Arrows*' ten aircraft, and a further twelve Gnats of 'C' Flight of the CFS, were detached to RAF Fairford, Gloucestershire in 1965. The following year they moved across to self-contained accommodation on 'G' site at RAF Kemble, just 10 miles to the west. They took advantage of the quieter circuit and used the end of Runway 13 as a parking area for the Gnats and any other visiting aircraft during the summer months.

In October 1966, the *Red Arrows* Gnats were cleared by the test pilots at Boscombe Down to use 'slipper' fuel tanks under their wings, enabling them to travel much greater distances. Up until then their range had been severely hampered by the fact that two of the integral fuselage tanks were adapted for storing diesel that, when injected into the exhaust, created the smoke.

Early 1967 saw the construction of a new aircraft-servicing pan opposite 'G' site specifically for the CFS detachment, and it was officially handed over in April. Shortly afterwards the *Reds* began returning from Little Rissington after their winter servicing programme, bearing the first signs of the relaxing of an Air Ministry ban on overzealous paint schemes. Through Ray Hanna's persistence the tail fins were painted red, white and blue, but the team had to wait another year before it was able to apply a white lightning stripe on the side of the fuselage.

▽ The team's colour change to red-painted Gnats early in 1965 brought about the new name the *Red Arrows*.

△ Popular nine-ship formations flown by the *Arrows* included this 'Concorde Bend' and the 'Diamond Pass'.

The Gnat was an extremely agile and quiet aircraft and this was a quality that all of its pilots enjoyed – especially the *Reds*. This allowed the pilots the chance to sneak over the Tetbury road across the airfield at very low-level, beating up the flight line or the runway controllers' caravan. Any unsuspecting members of the ground crew were then doused in the diesel fumes from the smoke and smelt the same for the rest of the day. In a game of dare, a couple of *Red Arrows* pilots took up a challenge to see who could fly the lowest through the 'V' shape formed by the roofs of the two 'G' site hangars, the winner being the one who deposited the most coloured dye on the surface. A very special bond between the *Arrows* (as they were always locally known) and Kemble village remains to this day. Long after they left, the *Arrows* would, if they were transiting the area, treat the villagers to a flypast, with their red, white and blue smoke trailing behind them, in recognition of that support.

In 1968, a team of nine pilots without reserves was approved. One of the newcomers that year was Flight Lieutenant Dickie Duckett, who recently described his experience to aviation journalist Ben Dunnell:

One of the requirements to be on the team was that you had to be a qualified flying instructor, which I wasn't at the time. I managed to persuade the team that I was a suitable person, and they said that if I thought I was, then I had to go and do the CFS course. So I applied for that, I did quite well, and at the end of it they said, 'Fine, you can join straight to the *Red Arrows*'. I was a bit late joining because I had to do that course first, and as I was the last pilot to join that year I was *Red 9*.

Something that was different in those days from the way the current team does it, and have been doing it for many years, was that the new guys joined the formation in the outside positions. Then as you got more experienced you worked in, so in my second year I became *Red 4*. These days, the new guys join on the inside, as *2, 3* or *4*, and work out as they become more experienced … Anyway, we started display flying about seven or eight weeks after I joined the team.

From the outset, Dickie realised that, as leaders go, Ray Hanna was something special. 'Ray Hanna was a wonderful man and a very skilled and experienced pilot,' he said. 'I certainly looked up to him and he was very much a sort of hero figure. He could do no wrong, he led the team brilliantly and I was very happy to follow him and do whatever he said was the right thing to do.' What made Ray's leadership so special was 'hard to define, really,' said Dickie:

He had an extremely good pair of hands and an absolutely wonderful natural ability to fly an aeroplane, a great feel for it. He also knew how to manage

▽ The long-range under-wing fuel tanks that could be carried after 1966 changed the Gnat's profile significantly.

⋀ An original red-painted Gnat lined up with the red, white and blue tail flash decorated aircraft at Kemble in 1967. *(via Glen Moreman)*

▷ Ray Hanna at very low level at Kemble. *(via Glen Moreman)*

flying in the weather and his past RAF Overseas Ferry Squadron service, delivering aeroplanes to units all round the world, had given him a great deal of experience of transiting an aeroplane from A to B at a time when today's sophisticated navigational devices just didn't exist. A lot of it was real 'seat of the pants' flying.

The qualities of the Gnat afforded exactly the precision required by the *Reds*, but it was not without its quirks, as Dickie explained:

I certainly found the business of learning to fly the Gnat in a formation aerobatic display quite challenging. The Gnat is a beautiful aeroplane to fly –

very small, of course, and you almost felt that you put it on when you got into the cockpit. You felt very much part of the aeroplane. I remember [Grand Prix driver] Jackie Stewart flying with Ray Hanna one day at Kemble in the winter; he was a qualified pilot, so I think Ray let him take the controls for a bit. He said it was just like being in a Formula 1 car with wings. It was extremely responsive, very light on the controls, very precise. It also had good engine response – you could go from full power to idle and back again quite quickly, and the rate of acceleration was very good.

We had a particular manoeuvre where, in a slightly opened-out arrowhead formation, we did a 'Twinkle' roll. I think the rate of roll was something like 450 degrees a second, so it went round very quickly. All you did was trim the aeroplane straight and level and apply full left aileron. In fact, the whole formation moved left about 10ft and down about 10ft, but, of course, because we all did it together it wasn't that obvious. There was an aileron restriction, and

the reason the roll rate was so high was to help with the slow handling on the approach, enabling you to have more powerful ailerons. Once you got above a certain speed that ability was ruled out by a switch, but we had got permission to prevent that happening, so that under certain in-trim conditions we could use full aileron at normal speed. That allowed us to do the 'Twinkle' rolls.

Ray Hanna had expected to relinquish the leadership task at the end of 1968, after a final display at the close of that year's Farnborough Air Show. He did leave, only to be asked back for 1969 after difficulties in off-season training.

▽ Gnats XR993 and XR977 taxiing for take-off to display at RAF Coningsby.
(Lindsay Peacock)

As Dickie Duckett remarked, 'Ray was quite a hard act to follow'. Even without notching up that still unequalled fourth consecutive year as *Red 1*, he had been awarded the 1968 Britannia Trophy, the citation reading: 'Under his brilliant leadership the standard of the *Red Arrows* has risen year by year until they are now generally regarded as the premier aerobatic team in the world.'

Through the 1970s the team had a succession of six leaders, with eight further pilots and a manager, the latter flying the 'spare' aircraft to displays and 'performing' as commentator. In 1973 the *Arrows* gave 103 public displays during the season, topping the century mark for the first time. The fuel crisis of 1974 prevented the team from giving public displays until July that year. The 1,000th performance came in 1977 at the International Air Tattoo at RAF Greenham Common. By the end of the 1979 season, when the Gnats were scheduled to be replaced by the new BAe Hawk T1, the team had given 1,292 public performances, involving visits to eighteen overseas countries.

Last year [1968] the announcer at an international air show said, as the Gnats started their display, 'Here come the *Red Arrows*, the best aerobatic team in the world' – and that is a very handsome tribute when you realise it was a French announcer speaking at a French air show.

GROUP CAPTAIN SIR DOUGLAS BADER

△ Biggin Hill Air Fair organiser Jock Maitland greets Ray Hanna on his arrival at the 1967 event. Note that the aircraft is in regular training livery as the leader had to borrow a 'standard' Gnat that day after an examination for structural checks grounded his usual red-painted aircraft.

▷ The *Red Arrows*, here reduced to seven aircraft because of the fuel crisis, displaying at RAF Chivenor in 1974.

△ Nine *Red Arrows* Gnats displaying at the Royal Netherlands Air Force sixtieth anniversary show at Deelen in 1973. (Inter-Air Press)

◁ Flying the popular 'Concorde Bend' formation.

△ The Battle of Britain Memorial Flight's Lancaster leading a fly-past with the *Red Arrows* in close formation. (Glen Moreman)

◁ Formation take-offs have always been a feature of *Red Arrows* displays.

△ *Red 1's* immaculate Gnat XS107 heading the line at the Bentwaters display in May 1973. (Lindsay Peacock)

▷ Seven Gnats making a spectacular 'Vixen Break'.

5 GNAT TO HAWK

The *Red Arrows* took delivery of the Hawk in the winter of 1979–80, setting the task of seeing through the conversion of the pilots from Gnat to Hawk. It introduced two new team members and worked up a display with a completely new aeroplane, in time for the start of the 1980 season. Ben Dunnell talked to Steve Johnson, who, as a flight lieutenant, joined the team towards the end of 1977 and went on to have a longer than normal four-year tour that bridged the Gnat and Hawk eras:

I joined the team, which was based at Kemble with Gnats, at the end of September 1977. I'd never flown the Gnat before, as my advanced flying training at Valley had been on the Hunter, so my first experience came when

they sent some QFIs from CFS and we had a few trips getting to grips with it before we started the aerobatic work-ups. I was put in the *Red 8* slot, back-right of the diamond. We had an accident in March when one of the new joiners was killed, so they brought back a previous team member. That was a bit of a hiccup at the beginning of your first season. In 1979, still flying the Gnat, I was put

▽ Hawks replaced Gnats by November 1979, and the *Red Arrows* flew the new aircraft the following season. (Daniel J. March)

into the *Synchro Pair*, so I did that season in the *Synchro 2* slot, which is *Red 7*. Of course, you do a season as *Synchro 2* and then become *Synchro* lead, *Red 6*. The big interest in this, as well as being *Synchro* lead and all the fun that involved, was that you were leader of the second section, so if we introduced a five-four split, as we did one year, you'd be leading the back four. With that in mind they 'froze' three of us, so I did another year as number two *Synchro*, as well as the *Synchro* leader, Richard Thomas, who subsequently became leader a few years later, and the leader, Brian Hoskins. We all marked time in our positions, and that's how I ended up doing four years total on the team.

My last flight on the Gnat was on 20 September 1979. By that time we'd finished the display season and positioned the Gnats around the country for their retirement.

Steve went on to say of the Gnat:

It was a delightful aeroplane – lots of vices, but it was great fun nevertheless. It was becoming increasingly expensive to maintain and operate and, as we were by then the last RAF Gnat unit, there were advantages of having commonality with the advanced jet trainer of the time. Plus, as the ambassadors and representatives of the Air Force, you really need to be demonstrating current equipment and modern types. The new trainer had been in service for a few years, and it was time to move on.

For the whole of the winter of '79 and early '80 we were consolidating, seeing what it would do and seeing what it wasn't quite so good at. There were plenty of advantages. For example, in the Gnat we had a radius of action for a full display of something like 35 miles. Quite often, if Synchro had been particularly harsh with thrust adjustments, we'd get through fuel quicker than the main guys. I remember a couple of displays in Germany operating out of Cologne where we actually had to leave the display before the end, because we were getting a little bit tight on fuel.

By contrast, looking at my logbook, with the Hawk we once took off from Kemble, transited to Naples and did a bit of an arrival display on getting there, which gives you an idea of the range and the flexibility. It is a very efficient aircraft. It has a bypass engine, the Adour, as opposed to the turbojet of the Gnat, the Orpheus, so fuel consumption was much better and the tankage was greater.

We started off wondering how we were going to fly the display, particularly on the *Synchro* side. I remember Richard Thomas and myself asking whether we should use the same parameters as we used with the Gnat, because we'd heard so much about the performance, and the turning performance in particular, of the Hawk that we thought it would exceed that of the Gnat.

△ Conversion through the winter of 1979 and the spring of 1980 led to the team's first public display with the Hawk in May 1980.

The Hawk could produce fantastic turn rates and was very manoeuvrable, but at higher speeds than we were flying in the team. It needed to be up at 400–450kt to really generate the turn rate and the G. In display work we were operating in the 300kt, plus or minus 50kt, range. 250kt was the lowest point, in what we used to call the undercarriage rollback, going up to 300, 320, 350 possibly for some of the looping manoeuvres – possibly not quite fast enough for the Hawk to demonstrate its full turning performance, when it was easily within the range of the Gnat.

The aerodynamic characteristics of the Gnat were very much 'swept-wing'. To explain, when you start approaching the stall in manoeuvre, you get a light buffet which you can feel in the airframe. When you approached that in the Gnat, there was still a lot of lift and manoeuvre left – in other words, if you

▽ The Hawk's different shape is highlighted in the 'Eagle Bend'.

△ A bigger aircraft presented a bigger 'picture' for the audience.

were getting fairly close to the ground and wanted to miss it, you could pull a great deal more into what we called the heavy buffet. It felt quite unstable, but the wing was still generating a lot of lift.

On the Hawk, it was a very efficient wing, but a bit more 'delicate' as a result. It had more of a straight-wing stall characteristic – in other words, the buffet margin was very, very narrow. As soon as you started feeling the buffet, there was a little bit more left, but if you pulled too much you were straight into the heavy buffet, it stalled and all the lift collapsed over the wing. Obviously, if you were pointing towards the ground thinking, 'I'm getting a bit close here', there wasn't much more margin.

We surprised ourselves, Richard and I, in the early days, replicating what we'd done in the Gnat in the Hawk. My recollection is that we started off adding 500ft to the vertical manoeuvres in the Hawk, and we ended up adding another 500ft. That was slightly disappointing, to have to add a greater margin than we'd expected. It was no reflection on the aeroplane, because, as I said, we were flying it slightly lower than its optimum speed. If we'd flown it faster, we'd have used a lot more display sky, a lot more airspace, and displaying in front of the crowd that wouldn't have looked so effective. Plus, we weren't displaying with flap, which in the Gnat generated a lot more coefficient of lift because the aerofoil camber changed quite significantly. It was a bit of an unfair comparison, really.

But there were so many positives to outweigh that. It was a bigger aeroplane, of course, so from the crowd's point of view there was an awful lot of metal in the sky when the 'Diamond Nine' came past you fairly close. The wing sweep was different from the Gnat, not quite so swept, so the geometry of the formation looked slightly different as well; some preferred it, some felt that the Gnat's wing sweep lent itself to the diamond formation slightly better.

For Steve Johnson, the 1980 season didn't get off to the best of starts when he had to eject from Hawk XX262 following a collision with a yacht mast during a seafront show at Brighton on 17 May. 'We were coming up for a cross,' he said:

I was descending, concentrating on the leader at that point to get the displacement correct and pick up his line, and the yacht in question had motored round without any sails on. In defence, you could say that if I had tried to look for it, his mast had been superimposed on the latticework of the Palace Pier. There was a big bang and the aircraft started rolling the wrong way. I was rolling left after the cross and it wanted to roll right straightaway.

According to the MoD accident report, the ejection, 'with the aircraft almost inverted and at no more than 300ft above the sea', was 'at the very limits of the seat's parameters'. It adds that there was 'no embargo on boat movements during the display and therefore no reason for the skipper of the yacht to suspect that his passage would hazard the *Synchro Pair*... In the circumstances, no blame was attached to the pilot.' Steve resumed display flying after a couple of weeks. It had an effect on the *Reds'* routine, though. 'We were cleared to 35ft above ground level with the Gnat,' he said. 'After my accident that was raised to 100ft.'

◁ The *Synchro Pair*, *Red 6* and *Red 7* performing the dramatic 'Carousel'.
(Kevin Storer)

6 REDS PILOTS

All *Red Arrows* pilots are volunteers. There are usually far more applications received than places available each year. A paper pre-selection reduces this to a shortlist of around nine. To be eligible for the team, pilots are required to have completed at least one operational tour on a front-line fast jet (such as the Tornado GR4 or Typhoon), and accumulated at least 1,500 flying hours. Current annual reports must have ranked them as being 'above average' in their flying role. Such provisos mean that the volunteers are usually Flight Lieutenants in their late 20s or early 30s.

The nine pilots selected for consideration are then attached to the *Red Arrows* for a short period. They meet the current team, fly in the back seat of the Hawks during display practice, and are then interviewed. At that stage the shortlisted pilots are deemed to be capable of meeting the professional high standard of flying that is required. The volunteers have also been assessed on their personal qualities, together with motivation. It is crucial that the nine display pilots in the team not only trust each other's skills, but also that they get on well.

▷ *Red 1* Squadron Leader Simon Meade (second left) with his three new team members in 1998 – Andy Evans (left), Andy Lewis (second right) and Dicky Patounas (right), who returned as leader in 2005.

◁ New team member flying in the back seat at the end of the season. (Jamie Hunter)

The current pilots then make the final choice at a 'closed' (no outsiders are ever permitted) meeting chaired by the commandant of the CFS. Unsuccessful candidates can reapply, provided they still meet the selection criteria. This whole process is, therefore, very democratic. Usually each of the display pilots stays with the team for a three-year tour of duty. By changing three pilots each year the experience level within the team is optimised. That is: three first-year pilots, three second-year pilots and three in their final year. The three new pilots normally join in the September to enable them to fly in the back seat with the team during the remaining displays of the season.

If a pilot goes sick during the display season, or for any other reason is unable to participate, the team is able to fly an eight-ship formation. For safety reasons there is never a reserve pilot. Team members always fly in the same position within the formation during that season.

When their tour is completed the pilots return to front-line squadrons to resume their mainstream career. A few leave the RAF at this stage to take up civil flying positions.

RED 1

The team leader, usually of squadron leader rank, will always have completed a three-year tour as a *Red Arrows* team pilot earlier in his career. The number of officers qualified for the position of leader is therefore quite limited.

Squadron Leader Jim Turner, the *Red Arrows'* twentieth leader, was the man tasked with taking the team into its fiftieth display season – 2014 being his third and final year as *Red 1*. Jim joined the RAF aged 18, after the award of a Royal Air Force Flying Scholarship. In the late 1990s his first squadron posting took him to RAF Coltishall, Norfolk. Here, he joined No. 41(F) Squadron, then equipped with the Jaguar GR3. Having become a qualified weapons instructor, he then transferred to No. 54 Squadron, still flying the Jaguar. Between 2000 and 2003, operational deployments took him to various parts of the world, including Iraq. The following year he became the RAF's 2004 season Jaguar display pilot, taking a specially marked aircraft to air show venues far and wide in its penultimate display season.

Flight Lieutenant Turner's successful application to join the *Red Arrows* resulted in him flying 2005's *Red 5,* under the command of Squadron Leader 'Dicky' Patounas. In 2006, he moved up to the *Synchro 2* position, thereafter becoming, in his last year, *Synchro Lead* under Wing Commander Jas Hawker's command. Now a squadron leader, Jim Turner then spent three years in the Middle East in an advisory role with the Royal Saudi Air Force's *Saudi Hawks* display team.

Immediately prior to rejoining the *Red Arrows* in 2012 as *Red 1*, Squadron Leader Turner was based at the Combined Air and Space Operations Center, in Qatar, working in support of Allied airpower sorties over Afghanistan. 'When I had to leave the Team in 2007 at the end of my three-year tour, I was sorry to have to go, but I knew it was right to let someone else have a go,' Jim reflected in 2013:

Four years later, sat in my living room at home shortly before heading off to the Middle East, I received a phone call from a very senior RAF Officer asking me if I would like to lead the *Red Arrows*. I was stunned. I accepted the offer and tried to sound calm and in control, but I think I sounded more like an excited schoolboy.

The experience of being team leader has been amazing. The type of flying I have to do is very different from the other pilots. I have to be as smooth and controlled as I can possibly be to allow the other eight aircraft to formate precisely on my aircraft. I find the pressure and responsibility of leading the team daunting and I am nervous before every display and flypast we do. I often wonder what I would say has been my most memorable moment flying with the *Red Arrows*. I have lots, but flying over the Olympic Stadium at the opening ceremony in 2012 was certainly one of the highlights.

◁ Eight Gnats displaying when a team member was temporarily unable to fly.

◁ Squadron Leader Dicky Patounas, who had previously flown as a team member in 1998–2000, was *Red 1* when the then Flight Lieutenant Jim Turner first joined the *Reds* in 2005. (Jamie Hunter)

▽ Taking the team into its fiftieth display season in 2014, Squadron Leader Jim Turner had rejoined the *Red Arrows* as leader in 2012. *(RAF Crown copyright)*

7 RED 10

The *Red Arrows* team manager, known as *Red 10*, is responsible for the smooth running of the team and for ensuring that the flying demonstration is well organised. In addition, he/she takes some of the workload from the team leader, the other team pilots and, to a lesser extent, the engineering tasks.

The overall planning of the display season is his primary task. Over the years many displays have been flown in support of the RAF Careers Information Service, and this may include the targeting of specific schools and areas. As for any major industry, the Royal Air Force aims to recruit 'the best'. Consequently the *Red Arrows* help encourage recruiting wherever they go.

Detailed planning for the first display begins about six weeks before the event, when logistics requirements are sent to the display organiser. The team manager maintains close contact with the organisers over the following weeks. Two weeks before each display a military operation order is issued showing timings, transit routes, personnel involved and any equipment required.

▽ Hawks arriving for a display with *Red 10*, the manager/commentator, flying the tenth aircraft.

The ten Hawks are usually flown to each operating airfield, the spare aircraft being flown by the manager, *Red 10*. The engineer officer and nine ground crew members fly in the rear seats of the aircraft during transit flights so that servicing can begin immediately on arrival.

Before the display, the pilots are briefed by the leader, who has to decide which sequences to fly according to the prevailing weather conditions. The manager normally gives the display commentary at each event. In some cases, such as the seaside shows, he has to be flown into the location by helicopter. In recent years *Red 10* has flown in a DHFS Squirrel helicopter based at RAF Shawbury.

The profound sense of *esprit de corps* which exists wihtin the *Red Arrows'* rank and file is unsurpassed in any other RAF unit, and this should come as no surprise. The exhilerating displays and the team's magnetic attraction are seen as a positive and highly succesful means of promotion for RAF recruitment.

RICHARD J. CARUNA

◁ Squadron Leader Andy Stewart, team manager 1989–91, giving the customary display commentary.

8 THE BLUES

The travelling ground crew, usually referred to as the *Blues* because of their blue suits, and known as the 'First Line', are a close-knit team of eighty-five dedicated and skilled tradesmen. Each is responsible for specific engineering tasks. They keep the *Red Arrows* show on the road by providing the wide range of support functions necessary to ensure the smooth running of the team.

Keeping the *Red Arrows* in the air is a complex, time-consuming process. Their working conditions are often difficult, with tasks having to be carried out quickly in order to prepare the Hawks for the next flight, allowing the performance of up to three displays in an afternoon.

The overall responsibility for the management of the *Blues* falls to the senior and junior engineering officers. The role of the senior engineering officer (SENGO) is the long-term management of the team's fleet of eleven aircraft. The junior engineering officer (JENGO) ensures that *Red 1* has sufficient aircraft to meet the daily task, whether that be training in winter or during the display season. Both officers are commissioned engineering officers selected for a two-year tour with the team, after which they leave to take up other engineering posts within the RAF.

△ One of the First Line *Blues* marshalling the leader to his parking slot at an air show.

△ The *Blues* move forward as the Hawks prepare to taxi for departure after displaying in Belgium.

⋀ *Reds* support C-130K Hercules arriving at Biggin Hill in June 1993.

▽ Occasionally the travelling ground crew has to carry out a significant task while deploying away from base. Here the pilots' ejector seat is being removed at an event in South Africa.

Nine of the tradesmen and the engineering officer are in the 'Circus', which means they each fly as a rear-seat passenger in the Hawk on transit flights. These are selected each December to form the select team for the following year. Each Circus member works with the same pilot throughout the season and is responsible for the aircraft's flight servicing, as well as the preparation of the pilot's flying kit.

Equally as important as the Circus are the remaining members of the First Line, who travel by road (or by support C-130 Hercules on overseas deployments if available). They provide the specialist support needed to rectify any minor faults that occur en route or during the display – and it is at these times that they really come into their own.

During the winter months First Line is somewhat scaled down to half-strength, operating what is known as 'Winter Line'. The remainder of the First Line moves across to the Second Line to assist with the winter servicing of the team's Hawk aircraft.

In the space of six months from October to March, the aircraft are given an extensive overhaul, which takes between four and sixteen weeks to complete. With the aircraft dismantled all systems are inspected and tested. This ensures that any faults are rectified before the next display season commences.

By the end of January, First Line is back to full strength, and all tasks for the coming display season have been allocated. This is a very intensive build-up period during which the new general support crews work up to speed for the following season. This allows time to perfect the operating procedures for the new season.

9 TECHNICIANS

Throughout the display season the rectification ground crew provides the diagnosis skill and practical expertise to maintain the aircraft between detachments. These technicians offer a variety of trades and specialist knowledge of propulsion, airframe, electrical, weapons and avionics. In addition there are some technicians from the survival equipment trade.

There are often only a few days between detachments, during which all the aircraft must be restored to pristine condition and prepared for the next deployment. Should an aircraft develop a serious problem whilst detached, a team of technicians from the rectification crew are quickly despatched to recover it.

Although the Hawk is a reliable, robust aircraft, there are inevitably items that need to be replaced. This responsibility falls to the team's suppliers. The team also has a fleet of fifteen vehicles, with its own section of drivers, who can operate everything from a refuelling bowser to a large articulated tractor and trailer.

▷ An Adour turbofan receiving attention from the engine technicians at RAF Scampton.
(Rolls-Royce)

The *Red Arrows* leader controls the display from start to finish and appears to fly the team as one. Throughout he flies smoothly and accurately, whilst positioning his manoeuvres within the confines of the display site. To him it feels like flying a very large cumbersome aircraft through a fighter tactics pattern, for, regardless of their place in formation, the pilots must maintain position.

This accurate positioning is achieved by the pilots' own considered judgement, and this expertise comes only with constant practice. The leader too is displaying his team by 'eyeball' judgement and will only use his instruments to achieve his desired aerobatic entry and exit speeds, and to maintain his sequence pattern. Even then it is usual for him to refer only to his air speed indicator, altimeter and power instruments.

It is essential that each of the sequences are memorised in full, not only by the leader but by all of the pilots. From the commencement of the display until completion some twenty minutes later there are more than twenty formations, manoeuvres and multiple formation changes. There are also synchronised items and upwards of thirty smoke 'on' and 'off' calls. Throughout the selected sequence the team is in close radio contact with each other, and the leader gives all advisory and executive commands.

◁ Pilots maintain their position in close formation by constantly watching the aircraft ahead of them. (Jamie Hunter)

▷ The leader controls the display from start to finish and appears to fly the nine Hawks as one. (Jamie Hunter)

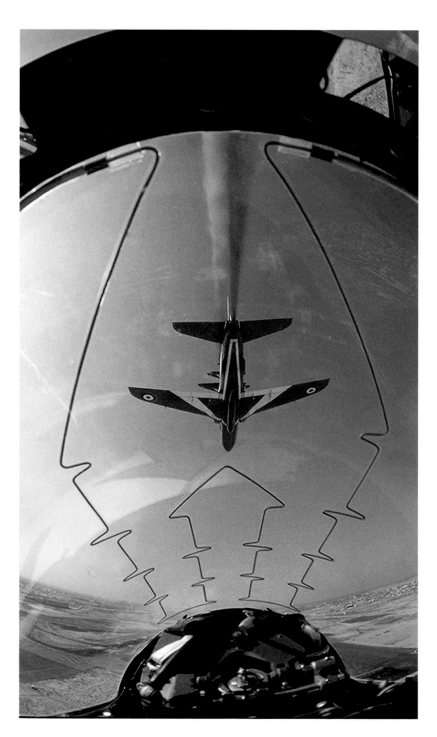

Team members acknowledge orders only when they are required to move to make a formation change.

Reds 1–5 form the front section known as *Enid*, and the *Reds 6–9* are known as *Gypo*. *Reds 6* and *7* are the *Synchro Pair* that performs the stunning manoeuvres during the second half of the display sequence. Over the years many different display formations have been flown by the team. The one constant, from the time that the *Red Arrows* was authorised to fly nine aircraft, is the trademark 'Diamond Nine' formation. Other favourite shapes and manoeuvres include 'Swan', 'Apollo', 'Lancaster', 'Tango', 'Big Battle', 'Short Diamond', 'Eagle', 'Chevron', 'Champagne Split', 'Cyclone', 'Goose', 'Heart', '*Gypo* Pass', 'Vertical Break', 'Corkscrew', 'Caterpillar', 'Mirror Roll,' 'Rollback', '*Gypo* Break', 'Vixen', 'Viggen', 'Carousel', 'Parasol Break', 'Clover', 'Split' and 'Typhoon'.

◁ A pilot's-eye view as the Hawks fly in line-astern, each maintaining their exact position. (Katsuhiko Tokunaga)

▷ *Reds 6* and *7*, the *Synchro Pair*, split to perform opposition passes.

△ 'Arrival Big Nine'.

△ 'Short Diamond' flypast. (Jamie Hunter)

◁ 'Swan'.

▷ 'Flanker'.

△ 'Goose'.

▷ 'Rollbacks'.

◁ *'Enid/Gypo* Crossover'.

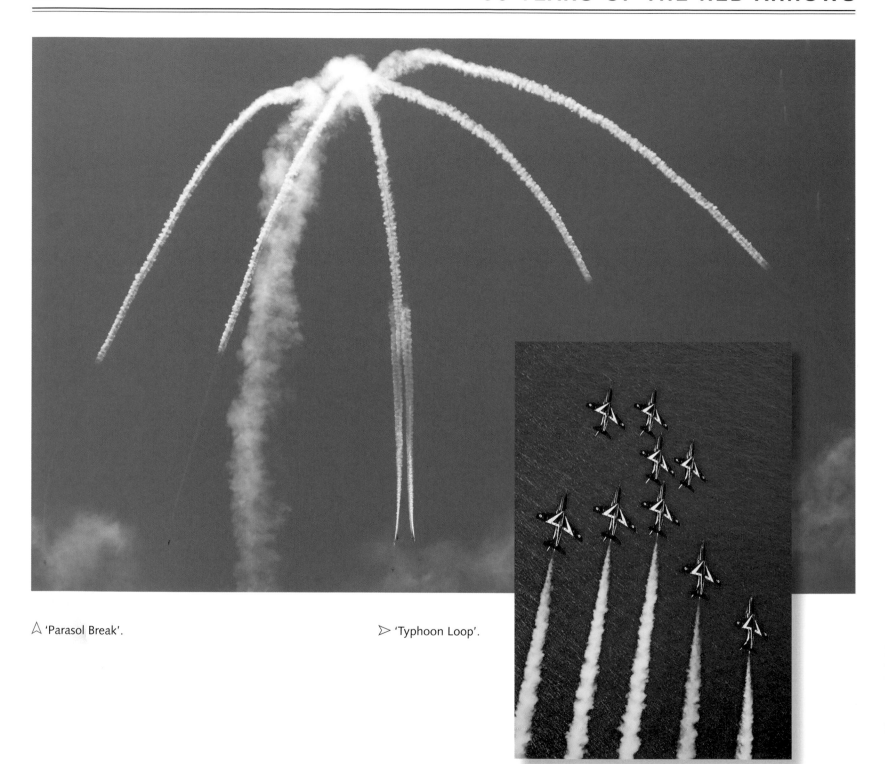

△ 'Parasol Break'.   ▷ 'Typhoon Loop'.

△ *'Synchro Pair* Heart'.

▷ *'Big Vixen Roll'.* (Paul Fiddian)

◁ 'Diamond Nine Loop'. (Kevin Storer)

◁ 'Spag Break'.

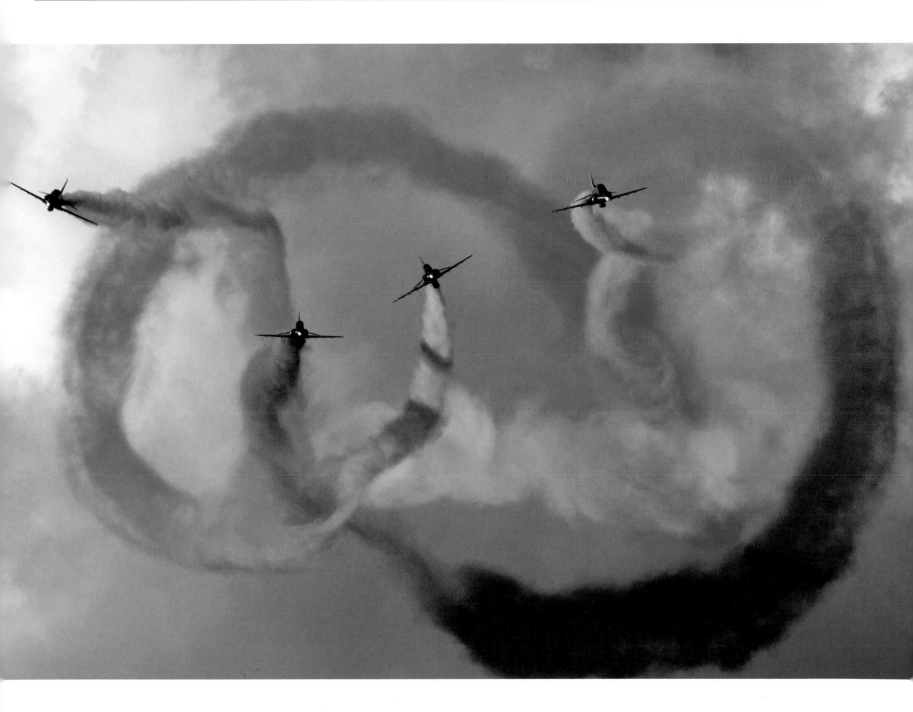

△ 'Gypo Break'.

△ 'Enid Rollback'.

▷ 'Bomb Burst'.

11 FLAG WAVING

Once equipped with the more versatile Hawk with its greater range, the *Red Arrows* were able to travel more widely, not only in Britain and Europe, but also on major tours to North America, the Middle East and Scandinavia. The first tour to the Far East was completed in 1986. It involved giving twenty-two displays in fifteen countries and travelling 18,500 miles in six weeks. Primarily the team performs the function of representing the Royal Air Force at individual air events around the world, but it has also increasingly promoted 'British excellence', especially the very successful Hawk aircraft, which has been developed and remains in production by BAE Systems today.

The *Red Arrows'* twenty-eighth season in 1992 was typical of the team's hard work at home and abroad, adding ninety-three displays that year. After a long winter's training, the *Arrows* detached to Akrotiri, Cyprus, for the annual Exercise *Springhawk*, with final practice and seeking formal clearance to display by the air officer commanding-in-chief, RAF Support Command. This secured, Squadron Leader Adrian Thurley led the team, for his second season, into the first three full public shows at Paphos, Akrotiri and Limassol on 25 and 28 April 1992.

Returning to the UK, the *Red Arrows* were soon into full swing with opening displays at Middle Wallop on 9–10 May and Abingdon on 15 May. The second of the seven overseas countries visited by the *Red Arrows* in 1992 was Spain, where the team operated from Rota to give a well-received display at the Expo '92 site at Seville on 21 May. After returning for the major Spring Bank Holiday shows at Mildenhall and Southend, it was off again, this time to Vaxjo, Sweden, for what had become an annual trip to Scandinavia.

Most regions of the UK get a visit from the *Arrows*, 1992 being no exception. Displays were given at Prestwick and Leuchars (Scotland), Douglas (Isle of Man), St Athan and Brawdy (Wales), Newtownards (Northern Ireland), Jersey and Guernsey. Major air shows, like the RAF Benevolent Fund's Air Tournament International at A&AEE Boscombe Down and the

▷ Opening their display at Southend-on-Sea, the *Red Arrows* fly past in 'Diamond Nine'.

Farnborough Air Show, were attended by Europe's premier jet display team; likewise some of the major sporting events such as the British round of the Formula One Grand Prix at Silverstone, saluting (on 12 July) Nigel Mansell's great achievement on his way to winning the World Championship. On the following day, 13 July, it was a sad final display at RAF Kemble, the team's former base for many years, which closed soon afterwards.

The first of two visits to Belgium in 1992 was unfortunately hit by poor weather, limiting the team to a flat display at Koksijde on 5 July. After a mid-season break at the beginning of August the *Red Arrows* visited their fifth overseas country. The two displays in Malta, the team's first visit to the George Cross island for fourteen years, were to commemorate the fiftieth anniversary of the Second World War siege of the island. Commenting on return from the visit, the *Red Arrows*' team manager, Squadron Leader Les Garside-Beattie, said that it was 'one of the best received overseas visits ever. Our entire 1992 publicity stock would not, had we been able to take it with us, been enough to satisfy the people of Malta.'

The traditional round of seaside displays from Whitby to Fowey kept the team busy for the remainder of August, which ended with a performance at the Great Warbirds Air Display at the event's new site, the Science Museum airfield at Wroughton, Wiltshire, and yet another new UK display location for the *Arrows*. Into September, and what was to be one of the year's highlights for the team, the first visit to Czechoslovakia took place; it was the forty-second foreign country that the *Red Arrows* have displayed in. It was also the last visit, as Czechoslovakia divided at the end of the year into two separate countries, the Czech Republic and Slovakia.

The venue for the two-day Czech and Slovak International Air Fest '92 was Ivanka civil airport at Bratislava, now the capital of Slovakia. The participants from all over Europe arrived on Thursday 3 September, ready for the public displays on Friday and Saturday 4–5 September and departure on Sunday 6 September. This allowed the *Red Arrows* to give a further display at Beauvechain in Belgium on the way home to Scampton. A Hercules C3 from No. 24 Squadron at Lyneham was tasked to support the tour, carrying the spares back-up, tools, smoke dye and all the other essential equipment needed away from base, along with eighteen of the *Blues* technicians. The remaining tradesmen flew as 'back-seaters' in the Hawks.

Recognising the importance of this first visit to Czechoslovakia by the *Red Arrows*, the commandant of the Central Flying School, Air Commodore Gordon McRobbie, headed the deployment, flying out one of the Hawks in place of *Red 4*, who was suffering from an ear problem and did not want to fly at high level for the transit. With the pilot's brief from team leader

Squadron Leader Adrian Thurley completed in his customary precise and detailed way, the ten Hawks were all set for their 10.04 a.m. departure on a fine, sunny morning. After the inevitable arrival procedures, both formal and social, the pilots and ground crew were driven into Bratislava. For many it was their first encounter with the relative austerity and warm friendship of this former Eastern bloc country. This was underlined at the evening meal taken at a large military high school in the town, which clearly had little place in the post-communist country. The day's work was not over for the *Red Arrows*' leader and team manager, who were invited to an air show press conference with the other teams and ended up doing a long TV interview.

In contrast to the warm sun for the arrival, the first day of the air show dawned grey, damp and cold. With the majority of scheduled airline traffic suspended for the duration of the flying display, the Czech and Slovak Air Force organisers were able to take over most of the large airport terminal building. The very thorough briefing, attended by all of the solo display pilots and aerobatic team leaders, was given by the CSIAF '92 organising team led by Colonel Pavel Strubl, deputy commander of the CSIAF. It was at this meeting that it was decided to call all the aerobatic team pilots together for a unique photograph, and the seeds of an idea to fly a formation of a representative aircraft from each of the teams were planted.

The air show opened on time at 11.00 a.m. and for the next seven hours, with light rain falling from a 6,000ft cloud base, there was a procession of top-class displays from ten countries in addition to the host nation. The first formation team was the CSIAF's unusual quartet of L-410 twin turboprop light transports, which was followed by the *Biele Albatrosy* – the *White Albatros* flying six white-painted L-39C Albatroses. In turn the Spanish *Patrulla Aguila*, Italian *Frecce Tricolori* and the *Patrouille de France* all took to the air, interspersed between solo displays from many different types. The final national team display slot fell to the *Red Arrows*, who were able to give a full aerobatic performance in improving conditions, producing spontaneous applause from the appreciative audience when they made their final break.

Although the second day was dry it posed even greater problems for the pilots as the cloud was lower and there was a strong, gusty wind, but the aerobatic teams all gave their performances. At the end of the air show, in a final salute to this extraordinary international event, the leaders of the six aerobatic teams took to the air for a series of unrehearsed fly-pasts. Unthinkable just a few years ago, a CSIAF L-39C Albatros led an RAF Hawk T1A and an Italian AF Aermacchi MB-339A on its port wing and a French AF Alpha Jet and a Spanish AF CASA Aviojet on its starboard, with a Russian Sukhoi Su-27P Flanker tucked tightly into the box.

This second day of the two-day Belgian Air Force International Airshow was attended by a very large crowd who were able to enjoy a good mix of military and civilian items, including the *Patrouille de France* which, like the *Red Arrows*, had hotfooted it from Bratislava. After a faultless display by the *Red Arrows*, which brought the crowd to their toes and produced a crescendo of applause when they had finished, the ground team made a rapid turn round and within an hour, and before the air show had finished, they were winging their way home to Scampton, with the support Hercules in ponderous pursuit. Of course there was more work to be done by the ground crew once they were back at base; all of the spares and equipment had to be unloaded from *Fat Albert* and returned to the appropriate stores – another hour's work.

△ *Red 1*'s Hawk in a unique formation led by a CISAF L-39C Albatros, with an Italian AF MB-339A, French AF Alpha Jet, Spanish AF Aviojet and a Russian Sukhoi Su-27P Flanker at Bratislava in September 1992.

▷ A spectacular view of the *Red Arrows* displaying at Dubai while en route to South Africa. (Peter Mobbs)

to fly for the Queen Mother when she visited Scampton to present a new Queen's Colour in June. It poured with rain all day long. The highlights for me were Expo '92 in Spain, where the eyes of the world were on us; the near-fanatical reception we received in Malta and the warmth of our reception in Czechoslovakia.

Since 1965, the *Red Arrows* have performed worldwide, flying well over 4,500 displays at home and abroad and have displayed in the following fifty-five countries: Australia, Austria, Bahrain, Bangladesh, Belgium, Brunei, Bulgaria, Canada, Cyprus, Czech Republic, Denmark, Egypt, Eire, Finland, France, Germany, Gibraltar, Greece, Hungary, Iceland, India, Indonesia, Italy, Japan, Jordan, Libya, Luxembourg, Malaysia, Malta, Monaco, Morocco, Netherlands, Norway, Oman, Pakistan, Philippines, Poland, Portugal, Qatar, Romania, Russia, Saudi Arabia, Singapore, Slovakia, Slovenia, South Africa, Spain, Sweden, Switzerland, Thailand, Turkey, Ukraine, UAE, USA and Zimbabwe.

⊿ Unloading support equipment from the Hercules back at Scampton.

Into the final four weeks of the 1992 season and the *Red Arrows* made their traditional appearances on the three public days at the Farnborough Air Show, followed by the Battle of Britain displays at Jersey and Guernsey and what should have been key performances at Leuchars and Finningley on 19 September. However, poor weather at the Scottish base restricted the team to a flat display and persistent fog for much of the day prevented them from even reaching Finningley. The weather improved the following day for the Cranfield Airshow, where the team made a nostalgic fly-past with the RAF's Vulcan to mark the V-bomber's retirement as well as giving their own impeccable final UK performance of the season.

The *Red Arrows*' last overseas visit in 1992 was to Gibraltar for the RAF station's open day on 26 September. The team had an unusual variation to their programme on 29 September. This was a fly-past from London to Dundee, overflying the major towns on the way, to mark the twenty-fifth anniversary of BBC Radio 1. A live commentary was broadcast from *Red 1* by Noel Edmonds, who flew with Adrian Thurley.

Looking back on his first season as manager of the *Red Arrows,* Squadron Leader Les Garside-Beattie commented:

It was a very busy but highly successful season for the team, only marred by some atrocious weather. Our biggest disappointment was not being able

⊿ The Queen Mother with the *Red Arrows* pilots at Scampton in June 1992 after presenting a new Queen's Colour to the team. (RAF Scampton)

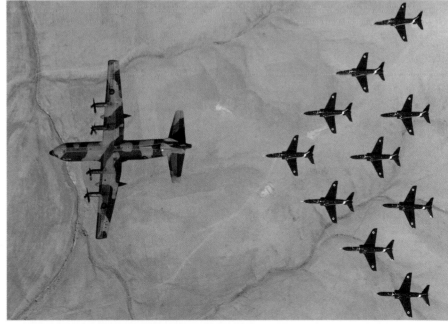

△ Dramatic view of the team looping over Victoria Falls during the visit to southern Africa in 1995. (Air Commodore Simon Bostock)

▽ In autumn 2002 the *Red Arrows* made a formation flypast over Niagara Falls with the Canadian *Snowbirds* team.

▷ *Eastern Hawk*, a Far East tour in July 1986, involved twenty-two displays in fifteen countries. The team here transiting Saudi Arabia with support Hercules. (BAe Military Aircraft)

◁ One of the more difficult European display venues is Switzerland. Here the team is shown at Sion, where high mountains surround the airfield on all sides.

▽ The *Reds* maintain their precise formation as they taxi in after a display in Spain.

◁ There is no mistaking where the *Reds* are flying in this photograph. During *Eastern Hawk '03* they visited ten countries including Egypt. (BAe Military Aircraft)

△ The team replaced the USAF *Thunderbirds* at the Wings over Houston Air Show at short notice during the 1993 North American tour.

▽ Team leader Squadron Leader Adrian Thurley signing autographs on the Fort Worth, Texas, crowd line.

▷ As the team flies over the Mediterranean, the formation's smoky shadow is reflected below one of the Hawks. (Action Air Images)

12 AIRBORNE AT SPRINGHAWK

To refine the skills of the team, the *Red Arrows* annually migrate to the Sovereign Base Area of the popular RAF station at Akrotiri in Cyprus. There they are able to make the most of the fine Mediterranean weather for intensive pre-season training, known as *Springhawk*. While in Cyprus the team embarks on a typically exhausting schedule, flying three full display practices every day of the working week to fine-tune the manoeuvres.

The whole team works hard to ensure that all of the Hawks are on the line in the morning, ready to make the most of the day's flying. Every member of the team works flat out to ensure the time spent there is maximised. In the air, the work rate for the pilots is extraordinary. The dark visors of the nine pilots conceal the immense concentration and workload exerted to stay on the wings of the leader as they paint the sky with red, white and blue smoke while looping, rolling and breaking. 'Good show' comes the call from *Red 10* on the ground as they complete the finale, the 'Vixen Break'.

Following each display, the pilots immediately go into a detailed debrief, making full use of the excellent video that is filmed from the ground during every performance. This is a vital tool for the pilots and they are typically hard on themselves – calls of 'short', 'long', 'shallow', 'deep' from various members of the team indicate how they feel their positioning is within each formation. It is this detailed debriefing that ensures the extraordinary levels of excellence the *Red Arrows* maintain.

Before displaying in public the team has to obtain a Public Display Authority – the legal permission for them to carry out displays in public. This is given by their commander-in-chief, at the end of the spring training camp, when he is satisfied the team has reached the required standard. At that stage the pilots move from normal flying suits to the traditional red suits. Soon afterwards they commence up to 100 public flying displays in the summer season, which concludes in the following September.

Jamie Hunter describes the never to be forgotten experience of flying with the team during *Springhawk* at RAF Akrotiri.

'I'm in the back Jamie?' Flight Lieutenant Damian 'Damo' Ellacott, in his first season with the team flying *Red 3* on the leader's left wing, comes up on the intercom, as he powers up the Hawk for my first flight this *Springhawk* with the team. '*Reds* check, 2, 3, 4, 5, 6, 7, 8, 9. Akrotiri tower *Red Arrows*, nine aircraft ready to taxi'. As Squadron Leader Patounas, the 'Boss', checks us in on the radio, I put my visor down and raise my oxygen mask as Damo checks I am ready for the canopy to close.

As we snake in order behind the Boss to runway 10 at Akrotiri, Damo gives me the safety brief regarding what is planned if we have a problem on take-off. I am happy in the back and the adrenaline is already starting to flow – and I am just a passenger here taking photos. 'Display take-off coming left', the call from the leader comes as we line up at intervals along the runway. '*Reds* rolling … now'. Power on, the pilots release the brakes and we roll as one. With my feet sitting lightly on the rudder pedals, the inputs come fast from my pilot as he keeps the Hawk arrow-straight on the runway.

Once airborne the nine Hawks move into tight diamond formation immediately – this is so close and the positioning is rock solid formation flying – the pilots are already working incredibly hard. A balance of power, airbrake, rudder and stick are what these highly skilled pilots use to hold this tight position, and it is very impressive from my position as a passenger. Squadron Leader Patounas calls *Red 10* Flight Lieutenant Andy Robins on the ground: 'Nine aircraft ready to display.' We are cleared in to a flat practice display over the cliffs at Akrotiri. 'Smoke on … go!' is the familiar call from *Red* leader as we begin our first pass over the cliffs practice display line at Akrotiri. 'Coming right … now. Holding the bank … now. Tightening.' The calls from the front of the formation are constant and they are vital. The team leader's skills guide the team safely around the routine and ensure positioning and timing and have so many factors to take into account, not least a strong on-crowd wind today.

For the first half of the flat display it is a sequence of turns in changing formations, 'Typhoon', 'Concorde', 'Short Apollo' to name a few. The work rate for the pilots is extraordinary throughout the entire flight. At what seems like just feet above the dark blue of the Mediterranean they are flying to the

⋀ Lining up ready to go in the Cyprus sunshine during *Springhawk* training.

⋀ Thumbs up from the back-seat passenger. (Jamie Hunter)

⋀ On the roll. (Jamie Hunter)

⋀ Airborne in close formation. (Jamie Hunter)

⋀ Pulling up into a loop. (Action Air Images)

⋀ Rock-solid formation flying. (Jamie Hunter)

⋀ Rolling above the Akrotiri runway. (Jamie Hunter)   ⋀ Nine *Arrows* over the top of a loop. (Jamie Hunter)

△ *Enid* breaks away from *Gypo*. (Action Air Images)

tightest of margins, lining up flap struts and other features on different parts of the aircraft in front to ensure perfect formation alignment.

The end of the first half of every display is marked by the team splitting into two sections – *Enid* and *Gypo*. *Enid* comprises *Reds 1–5*, with *Gypo* being formed by *Reds 6–9*. The second half of the display contains manoeuvres which are much more dynamic with the aim being to keep something happening in front of the crowd at all times. This involves a series of co-ordinated manoeuvres for the two sections including *Gypo* section's famous *Synchro* crossing manoeuvres, led by *Red 6*, *Synchro* leader Flight Lieutenant Si Stevens.

For this display I am with *Enid* and both sections fly back to the crowd line with highly accurate timing to keep the action in front of the crowd but also to ensure deconfliction between the two sections. We fly the 'Goose', involving a deep Vic formation of our five *Enid* Hawks being literally 'goosed' by Flight Lieutenant Dave Slow in *Red 8* – flying fast between us. This is followed by 'Twinkle' aileron rolls, 'Rollbacks', and the display culminates with the 7G pull of the 'Vixen Break'. The 'Rollback' looks relatively benign from the ground – in the cockpit the aileron roll seems incredibly violent, but at the same time smooth and controlled, and over in a fraction of a second!

After thirty minutes we are running in for the break over the runway. One last G-saturated pull and we are downwind for landing in sequence. A quick check from Damo that my toes are clear of the brakes and we turn finals and we grease down on the runway at Akrotiri. The sweat is pouring off me, so goodness knows how the pilots have remained so cool. As we taxi in I am cleared to replace my ejector seat and canopy safety pins and we come to a halt as we are met by the dedicated ground crews. As the canopy opens, the engines have already spooled down and Damo is already climbing out. 'See you inside,' he says. Now the engineers swing into action to prepare the jets for the next practice, while the pilots head off for their detailed debrief.

▽ Pilots are working hard to maintain the tight formation through the manoeuvres. (Jamie Hunter)

▷ Vertical into the 'Parasol Break'. (Jamie Hunter)

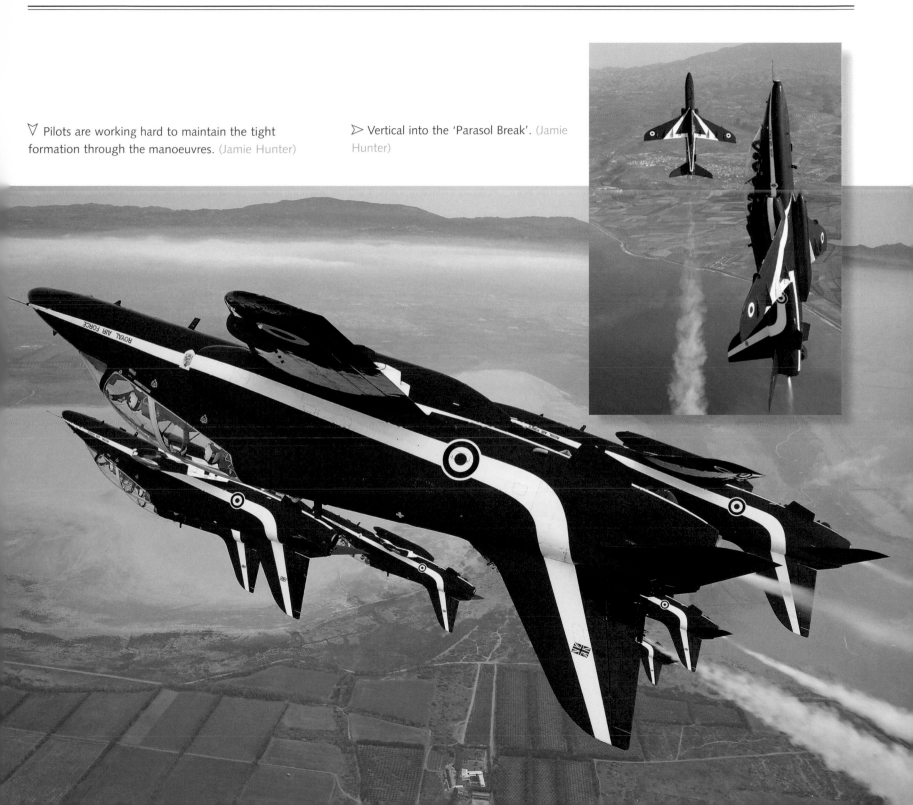

△ Airbrakes out to slow the Hawks' speed during a tricky break. (Jamie Hunter)

◁ Over the top in 'Apollo'. (Jamie Hunter)

▽ Pulling 7G in the 'Vixen Break'

13 JOINING THE TEAM

Flight Lieutenant Kirsty Moore attracted a lot of attention when, in 2010, she became the first female pilot to make the grade as one of the nine red-suited display pilots. She flew as *Red 3*, with her fellow newcomer that year Flight Lieutenant Ben Plank flying as *Red 2* on the opposite side of the 'Boss', Squadron Leader Ben Murphy.

Recounting her RAF career, Flight Lieutenant Moore said:

Once I had completed flying training I remained at RAF Valley as a 'Creamie' instructor on the Hawk. That meant that after I finished my training they decided to train me up as an instructor to teach the new students. I subsequently moved to RAF Marham to join No. 13 Squadron as a Tornado GR4 pilot, and I flew there for three years. That tour saw me reaching 1,500 hours of fast jet flying and an operational front-line tour. I had also been assessed by my squadron commander as being above average, which together meant that I had the qualifications I needed to apply for the *Red Arrows*.

I submitted my application to the team, but as it was my first attempt I did not hold out much hope and was doing it with a view to seriously applying for the 2011 season. Showing your face for a year is not a bad thing to do, with a hope of getting into the team the following year. That mindset meant that I did not put myself under too much pressure during the shortlist selection week in Cyprus. That was exactly what worked out so well and I got in!

⋀ During winter training, the new team members take to the air at least three times each day (weather permitting) as they develop and hone their formation flying skills. (Jamie Hunter)

△ Flight Lieutenant Kirsty Moore climbing out of the cockpit of the Hawk and heading back with Flight Lieutenant Ben Plank to debrief after a sortie at Scampton. (Jamie Hunter)

Kirsty's team-mate Flight Lieutenant Ben Plank, who joined the team at the same time, relished his new role:

It is a tough regime and very different from what I was used to flying the Harrier operationally. The *Reds* fly three times a day, five days a week and each sortie brings new challenges. So it's been an incredibly intense, but hugely rewarding, experience as we learnt to fly our positions in the formation, master the basic manoeuvres and begin to put the display together in carefully managed building blocks. It is non-stop all day but it is fantastic, with superb flying, striving for perfection, and all-consuming. I even dream about *Red Arrows* manoeuvres! There's not a single part of the day when I'm not thinking about the display. Sometimes if something is not quite working out for us I can go to one of the experienced third-year pilots and ask them to fly in the back seat of my jet to see why I'm not picking something up. Once we got

our positions for the 2010 season I immediately started flying in the back seat for the rest of last year with *Red 2*, Zane Sennett.

Kirsty Moore describes some of the new skills she quickly learnt:

For our first sortie I was hoping that we'd be flying with someone in our back seat telling us what we needed to do. But no. Planky [Ben Plank] and I had to fly with the Boss in a three-ship formation and we just went straight into it! We did a few left and right turns and then we went straight into flying loops. From that point everything has just ramped up. The training I am used to on the Hawk involved starting to input for a turn or a manoeuvre as you saw the flight leader move. Whereas here we do it all to the leader's voice commands. I like to call it 'voice activated' formation flying. When the Boss says 'coming left now', it's the 'now' that we react to.

The Hawk is very agile, almost twitchy until you're used to it. But it's actually very easy to fly smoothly. However, coming from the GR4 it took some re-adjusting. The Tornado is such a big, heavy aircraft that you could pretty much move the stick three inches to the side and the wings wouldn't move. Do that in a Hawk and you're all over the place! Our three trips each day meant that I was mentally exhausted. But you need to sleep well, so I actually go for a run to physically tire me out so I wake up fresh each morning.

With the *Red Arrows* I cannot plan anything – it's all about the thirty minutes when we are airborne. It's all about having the correct angle of bank, the correct spacing. Every second of the display is video taped and dissected in minute detail. No one ever looked at tapes of my flying in the GR4 and said 'your wings aren't level'! I'm very critical of myself for the full duration of the sortie. As a qualified flying instructor (QFI) my background is teaching circuits. I was also the QFI on No. 13 Squadron, so it was my role to ensure we all flew things like circuits correctly. But this is very different. Now we walk into our briefing pre-flight and it's backed right up against the sortie. As soon as I get into the brief I have to be on my game. When we taxi I am totally switched on. It's interesting that when you are getting used to concentrating for that length of time you think you are focussed but you're not – something happens that I haven't reacted to properly, and it's because I'm actually staring at the Boss – and I realise that I need to get even sharper.

As a kid I never thought of joining the *Red Arrows*, I never thought I'd be in a position where I was good enough or in the right place to try to do it. When I first joined the RAF I wanted to fly the Jaguar, but as I stayed at RAF Valley as an instructor I missed the Jaguar, as it was retired from service. A lot of people ask what it's like to be the first girl in the *Red Arrows*. Well there is no real answer for that. I know what it feels like to be in the *Red Arrows* – I just happen to be a girl. The publicity hasn't detracted from just being another member of the team and it's great that I've been able to carry on as normal.

⚠ It all comes together at *Springhawk* in Cyprus where the team receives its Display Authorisation and the pilots change into their familiar red flying suits for the season ahead. (Jamie Hunter)

14 DIFFICULT YEARS

2011 began much like any other *Red Arrows* year. With their Display Authorisation granted the team made its first UK appearance at the Southend Air Period on 29 May. Just under three months later, the *Red Arrows* appeared at the fourth annual Bournemouth Air Festival. In good weather conditions, Saturday 21 August's full beachfront display ended with the standard Vixen Break and, having regrouped, the team headed back to Bournemouth Airport. Splitting formation over the airport, each team member then joined the circuit and prepared to land. Flight Lieutenant Jon Egging, *Red 4*, did not touch down on Bournemouth's runway that day; sadly, he crashed approximately 1km beyond its boundary, with fatal results.

Not surprisingly the *Red Arrows* did not participate in the Bournemouth Air Festival's closing display, nor did they give any other performances that month. With a poignant eight-ship formation, the *Red Arrows*' 2011 display season resumed on 2 September. The Military Aviation Authority, having studied all the available data about the aircraft and the background to the crash, reported some months later that G-LOC (G-force induced Loss of Consciousness) appeared to have been the cause. Meantime, on 8 November 2011, a second fatal accident compounded the season's sense of tragedy. This involved an involuntary ejection from a Hawk on the ground at Scampton, followed by failure of the main parachute, which resulted in the death of *Red 5*, Flight Lieutenant Sean Cunningham. Never before had the *Red Arrows* lost two of its pilots in separate circumstances within a single year and, thus, the *Red Arrows*' forty-seventh display season ended on a very sad note.

▷ Squadron Leader Jim Turner led a reduced team of seven Hawks through the 2012 season.

In March 2012, Flight Lieutenant Kirsty Stewart (formerly Moore) announced her departure – a surprise decision apparently linked to the previous season's fatalities. 'Kirsty completed two immaculate seasons with the team, performing to a level expected of any *Red Arrows* pilot,' said *Red 1*, Squadron Leader Jim Turner, in a 10 March news release. 'She leaves the team with our thanks for her dedicated service and our best wishes for her future.' He added:

> The last few months have been the hardest that the team have endured for a long time, however; in true RAF spirit and ethos we are determined to put the recent tragedies behind us and move forward to promote our reputation as one of the finest, most professional and safest military display teams in the world.

Faced with the prospect of presenting an uneven, eight-ship formation that year, the *Red Arrows* downsized to a seven-ship, thereby limiting the

△ Seven Hawks in 'Big Arrow' formation at Fairford in July 2012.

involvement of *Red 8*, Flight Lieutenant Dave Davies, solely to high-profile flypasts. In 2012, such flypasts abounded and saw the *Red Arrows* participate in the Queen's Diamond Jubilee celebrations, along with the London 2012 Olympic Games Opening Ceremony and its Athletes' Parade. Flown with seven aircraft, 2012's displays began at Folkestone on 2 June. To accommodate the change, certain manoeuvres were dropped or reconfigured.

In June 2012, answering a long-standing question about the *Reds'* future home base, the MoD confirmed that Scampton would retain this role at least until 2020. Two months later, the team visited Russia for the first time in twenty-two years, participating in the Russian Air Force's massive centenary celebrations at Zhukovsky Air Base alongside multiple teams from the East and West.

15 FULL FLIGHT

Some doubted whether, in an age of heavy and regular defence cutbacks, the *Red Arrows* could ever again give displays with all nine aircraft. These fears were allayed when, in February 2013, the first nine-ship formation of the year was flown – the full *Red Arrows* were back! The first display of 2013 on 26 May – at the *Patrouille de France*'s sixtieth anniversary event at Salon de Provence, France – was thus a cause of much celebration. Triumphantly, all nine Hawks overflew the French crowd before pulling up to start the 'Arrival Loop' – a sight oft-repeated thanks to 2013's generally excellent summer weather. On 6 July, RAF Waddington hosted the *Red Arrows*' 4,500th display

– a season highpoint, followed a fortnight later by two unique flypasts at the Royal International Air Tattoo (RIAT) 2013 at Fairford. The first was accompanying British Airways' first Airbus A380 airliner on the Saturday and the following day with an Airbus A400M Atlas military transport aircraft, thereby showcasing the 'Best of British' and the RAF's future airlift capability.

Several weeks after the forty-ninth UK/European season came to an end with displays in Monaco and Malta, it was announced that the team had accepted an invitation to participate in the Dubai Air Show (17–21 November) and was to make a month-long visit to the Middle East

▷ Back to normal in May 2013 for a full season with nine Hawks. (Denis Calvert)

from 4 November. This major tour also included displays at the Al Ain Aerobatic Show in Abu Dhabi (30 November–2 December) as well as Qatar, Bahrain, Oman, Kuwait and visits to Jordan and Saudi Arabia. During the tour, which increased the total number of displays in 2013 to eighty, Flight Lieutenants Stewart Campbell and Joe Hourston, the *Red Arrows*' two new pilots for 2014, commenced their training.

We must give a big 'thank you' to all the *Red Arrows* pilots, ground crew and support staff for providing five memorable decades of superb displays at home and abroad. But as we look ahead we must also remember the ten pilots who lost their lives in six fatal accidents while members of this fantastic team.

△ Team line-up for 2013: eleven *Reds*, the engineers and *Blues*. (RAF, Crown copyright)

▷ British Airways' first Airbus A380 airliner made its public debut escorted by the *Red Arrows* on the first day of the Royal International Air Tattoo 2013 at Fairford. (Jamie Hunter)

△ On the second day of RIAT 2013 the *Reds* flew with an A400M Atlas transport in the display. (Jamie Hunter)

APPENDIX I
LEADERS
1965-2014

1965	Flight Lieutenant Lee Jones	1988–90	Squadron Leader Tim Miller
1966–69	Squadron Leader Ray Hanna	1991–93	Squadron Leader Adrian Thurley
1970	Squadron Leader Dennis Hazell	1994–96	Squadron Leader John Rands
1971	Squadron Leader Bill Loverseed	1997–99	Squadron Leader Simon Meade (Wing Commander in 1999)
1972–74	Squadron Leader Ian Dick	2000–01	Squadron Leader Andy Offer (Wing Commander in 2001)
1975–76	Squadron Leader Richard 'Dickie' Duckett	2002–04	Squadron Leader Carl 'Spike' Jepson
1977–78	Squadron Leader Frank Hoare	2005–06	Squadron Leader Richard 'Dicky' Patounas (Wing Commander in 2006)
1979–81	Squadron Leader Brian Hoskins	2007–09	Wing Commander Jas Hawker
1982–84	Squadron Leader John Blackwell	2010–11	Squadron Leader Ben Murphy
1985–87	Squadron Leader Richard Thomas	2012–14	Squadron Leader Jim Turner

⋀ Squadron Leader Tim Miller debriefing the pilots at Scampton in 1989.

⋀ Prior to a training sortie in March 1991, Squadron Leader Adrian Thurley (right) is in discussion with Flight Lieutenant Simon Meade (centre right) who returned to lead the team in 1997.

⋀ Squadron Leader 'Spike' Jepson (left), at Biggin Hill in 2004, receiving an award to mark the team's fortieth season from Jock Maitland (centre), with Ray Hanna, *Red 1* 1966–69, looking on.

APPENDIX II
GNAT AND HAWK

Folland (Hawker Siddeley) Gnat T1

Powerplant:	One Bristol Siddeley Orpheus Mk 100/101 turbojet of 4,230lb st (18.84kN)
Span:	24ft 0in (7.32m)
Wing Area:	150sq ft (16.26sq m)
Length:	31ft 9in (9.68m)
Overall Height:	9ft 7in (2.93m)
Max Speed:	Mach 0.95; 640mph (625kts/1,030km/h)/ Mach 1.15 in a shallow dive
Max Weight:	8,914lb (4,043kg)
Accommodation:	Two seats, in tandem

In November 1953, Bristol had begun to develop the Orpheus turbojet, because NATO liked the idea of a light fighter and ground-attack aircraft. The engine was a godsend for the Gnat, which first flew on 18 July 1955.

In August 1955, the Ministry of Supply placed an order for six Gnat fighters for development flying, but the type was not adopted by the RAF.

However, by the latter half of 1957, the Gnat's potential as a two-seat trainer was realised. An initial pre-production order was placed for fourteen aircraft. In February 1960, this was followed by an initial production order for thirty Gnat T1s.

The first Gnat T1 flew on 31 August 1959, and the type first entered service with the RAF at the Central Flying School at Little Rissington in February 1962. It replaced the Vampire T11 as the RAF's standard advanced trainer in Flying Training Command.

The first Gnat course at No. 4 (Advanced) Flying Training School began in early 1963. In the following year 4FTS formed its own aerobatic team with yellow-painted Gnats, known as the *Yellowjacks*. In 1965 they became the *Red Arrows*.

Gnats remained in service as the RAF's standard advanced trainer until replaced by the Hawk at RAF Valley in November 1978. The *Red Arrows* Gnats gave their last display at Valley on 16 September 1979.

◁ Gnats as flown by the CFS/4FTS (XM693 centre), the *Yellowjacks* (XR992 right) and the *Red Arrows* (XS111 left).

Gnats With The *Reds*

A total of twenty-eight Gnats flew with the *Red Arrows* during the type's fourteen years with the team. Though some aircraft were withdrawn from use while attached to the team, they were not necessarily struck off RAF charge. Several Gnats from No. 4 FTS Valley were attached to the *Red Arrows* early in 1968 (other team aircraft were cleared following the temporary grounding of the type and these are not included):

XP501, XP505, XP514, XP515, XP531, XP533, XP535, XP538, XP539, XP541,

XR537, XR540, XR545, XR571, XR572, XR574, XR955, XR977, XR981, XR986, XR987, XR991, XR992, XR993, XR994, XR995, XR996,

XS101, XS107 and XS111.

△ Gnat T1 XR987 landing at RAF Little Rissington in August 1972. (Denis Calvert)

Red Arrows Gnats Written Off in Accidents

XP501 Cr 13-06-1969, Fairford, Glos
XP531 Cr 16-02-1976, Kemble, Glos
XP539 Cr 22-05-1979, Leeming, Yorks
XR545 Cr 20-01-1971, Kemble, Glos after collision with XR986
XR573 Cr 26-03-1969, Kemble, Glos

XR981 Cr 03-03-1978, Kemble, Glos
XR986 Cr 20-01-1971, Kemble, Glos after collision with XR545
XR992 Cr 16-12-1969, Kemble, Glos after erroneous engine fire call
XR994 Cr 13-11-1970, Kemble, Glos
XR995 Cr 16-12-1969, Kemble, Glos after engine fire

Red Arrows Gnats – UK Survivors

XP505   Science Museum, Wroughton, Swindon, Wiltshire

XR537   (Registered G-NATY) Drilling Systems Ltd, Bournemouth Airport, Hurn, Dorset

XR571   RAF Scampton, Lincolnshire (displayed statically outside *Red Arrows*' HQ)

XR574   Trenchard Museum, RAF Halton, Buckinghamshire

XR977   RAF Museum Cosford, Shropshire

There are two Gnats that did not serve with the *Red Arrows* that are painted to represent *Yellowjacks/Red Arrows* aircraft, both operated by Heritage Aircraft at North Weald:

XS102   (Registered G-MOUR) Painted as *Yellowjacks* XR992

XP504   (Registered G-TIMM) Painted as *Red Arrows* XS111

In addition Gnat XP502 is preserved at Cotswold Airport/ Kemble painted to represent *Red Arrows*' Gnat XR540, the first red-painted aircraft to be delivered to the team at RAF Fairford on 1 February 1965.

△ Painted in *Red Arrows* colours as XS111, Gnat G-TIMM is operated by Heritage Aircraft at North Weald.

△ Gnat XP502, preserved at Kemble in front of the control tower, is marked to represent the first red-painted *Red Arrows* Gnat XR540.

△ Gnat G-MOUR (XS102) was painted in *Yellowjacks* colours with the serial XR991 from 1990 to 2010, and is now flying with Heritage Aircraft as XR992.

△ Gnats gave way to Hawks in the winter of 1979.

Hawker Siddeley (BAe) Hawk T1/T1a

Powerplant:	One Rolls-Royce/Turboméca Adour Mk 151 turbofan of 5,200lb st (23.16kN)
Span:	30ft 9.75in (9.39m)
Wing Area:	180sq ft (16.72m2)
Length:	39ft 2in (11.96m)
Overall Height:	13ft 1in (3.98m)
Max Speed:	622mph (1,000km/h) at sea level
Max Weight:	16,260lb (7,7374kg)
Accommodation:	Two seats, in tandem

The Hawk first flew in 1974, and entered RAF service on 4 November 1976, as both an advanced trainer and a tactical weapons training aircraft. It was designed to serve as a replacement for the Gnat and Hunter T7, as well as for some of the roles of the Jet Provost, in a major rationalisation of RAF training programmes from 1977 onwards. It is a strong and rugged trainer and has been designed to cut operating and maintenance costs, while achieving a long fatigue life. It was the first British aircraft to be designed from the outset using metric measurement.

A total of 175 Hawks entered service with the RAF. Flight tests demonstrated that the Hawk exceeded all of its performance requirements and, although supersonic speed was not specified, the prototype (XX154) exceeded Mach 1.04 in a shallow dive in February 1975.

The *Red Arrows* received eleven Hawks between August and November 1979 from the production aircraft for the RAF. They were modified with the smoke system and given the distinctive red, white and blue paint scheme. In other respects the Hawks flown by the team are in the same configuration and have been modified and upgraded in the intervening years in line with the rest of the fleet. Through the period of the Cold War the team's Hawks could be armed with 30mm cannon and Sidewinder air-to-air missiles and used to augment the UK air defence forces. More than three decades after the Hawk prototype's first flight, a much developed version, the BAE Systems Hawk T2, is in service with the RAF.

△ *Red Arrows* Hawks could be armed with a cannon and missiles to assist the UK's air defence force during the Cold War. (BAe Military Aircraft)

Red Arrows Hawks 1979-2014

Serials in bold are Hawks that were current with the team during 2013.

XX177, XX179, **XX219**, **XX227**, XX233, XX237, XX241, **XX242**, XX243, XX244, XX245, XX251, XX252, XX253, XX257, XX259, XX260, XX262, **XX263**, **XX264**, XX266, **XX278,** XX292, XX294, XX297, XX304, XX306★, XX307, XX308, **XX310**, **XX311**, **XX319** and XX320, **XX322**, **XX323** and **XX325**.

★ RAF Scampton gate 2014

▷ Hawk T1A XX227, which was still flown by the team in 2013, was one of the first to equip the *Reds* in 1979. *(Katsuhiko Tokunaga)*

Red Arrows Hawks Written Off in Accidents

XX179 Cr 20-08-2011, Throop, Dorset
XX233 Cr 23-03-2010, Kasteli, Crete
XX241 Cr 16-11-1987, after collision with XX259, Welton
XX243 Cr 22-01-1988, Scampton
XX251 Cr 21-03-1984, Akrotiri, Cyprus
XX252 Cr 17-11-1998, Scampton

XX257 Cr 31-08-1984, Sidmouth, Devon
XX259 Cr 16-11-1987, after collision with XX241, Welton
XX262 Cr 17-05-1980, Brighton
XX297 Cr 03-11-1986, Scampton
XX304 Cr 24-06-1988, Scampton
XX320 Cr 30-08-2008, Cranwell

FIVE DECADES

1965   1 February: Delivery to the CFS of the *Red Arrows*' first Gnat T1, XR540. This had also been the *Yellowjacks*' first aircraft.

1 March: The *Red Arrows* formally established at RAF Fairford with a total of eight pilots including Flt Lt Lee Jones as leader and a reserve pilot.

6 May: First media presentation by the *Red Arrows* at RAF Little Rissington.

9 May: The *Red Arrows*' first public appearance at Clermont-Ferrand during the French Air Force Meeting de l'Air.

14 May: The *Reds* received the last production Gnat T1, XS111, which brought the team's strength to nine aircraft (of which seven were used for displays, together with an airborne spare).

15 May: First UK public appearance of the *Red Arrows* at the Biggin Hill Air Fair.

At the end of the 1965 season, the Royal Aero Club awarded the *Red Arrows* its Britannia Trophy 'for the British aviator or aviators accomplishing the most meritorious performance in aviation history during the year'.

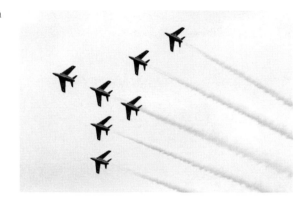

△ *Red Arrows* in 'Half Swan' formation at their first Uk public display at Biggin HIll on 15 May 1965.

△ XR540, here low and fast, was the first Gnat to be flown by the *Yellowjacks* and the *Red Arrows*.

△ *Red Arrows*' debut at Little Rissington, 6 May 1965, in a 'Vixen Pass'.

△ Flight Lietenant Lee Jones (kneeling) with the first *Red Arrows* team lined up in their formation positions in May 1965.

◁ In 1968 the *Red Arrows* were permanently established to display with nine Gnats.

▷The team lined up at a very wet RAF Turnhouse, Edinburgh, in June 1971.

1966   Sqn Ldr Ray Hanna became leader of the *Red Arrows* and performed eighty-five displays with them that year, including the SBAC Show at Farnborough.
The team made a tour of the Mediterranean, including Cyprus, Malta and Jordan.
8 July: First display with nine pilots.
6 August: First nine-ship display in the UK at RNAS Brawdy.

1967   The beginning of the 1967 season was delayed following grounding of all RAF Gnats after structural weaknesses were discovered in the tail units of some aircraft.
For the season the entire fin was painted in flashes of red, white and blue, with a Union Jack superimposed on the white segment.
Red Arrows reduced to seven aircraft.

1968   50th anniversary of the RAF. *Red Arrows* flew over 100 shows during the year.
The team was permanently increased in size to nine and the new 'Diamond Nine' Gnats formation became the team's symbol.

1969   Pilots' names were painted in white lettering below the canopies of the aircraft.
Previously a detachment of the CFS, the *Red Arrows* was established permanently as a standard RAF squadron.
12 December: The team's first aircraft loss. During practice, one aircraft caught fire; another team member radioed its pilot, who ejected, along with the pilot of another Gnat in the formation who 'banged out' in error.

1971   20 January: Tragic accident at RAF Kemble when two aircraft were lost and four pilots killed. This was the team's first fatal accident.

1972   17 May: The team embarked on its first US tour – Operation Longbow.

1973   13 June: An authenticated crowd of 650,000 people watched the *Red Arrows* display at Lisbon, a figure not exceeded until Sydney in 1996.

1974   Start of the display season postponed due to the worldwide energy crisis.

1975   The fuel crisis continued and only fifty-six displays were flown in the year.

1977   26 June: The 1,000th display by Gnats was performed at the International Air Tattoo at RAF Greenham Common.

1978   The white nose flash was 'broken' to accommodate the words 'Royal Air Force' in white lettering.

◁ A sick pilot meant an eight-ship display, which produced some unfamiliar Gnat formations.

1979   The first pre-season training camp was held at RAF Akrotiri, Cyprus.

August: First BAe Hawk aircraft was delivered to the *Red Arrows* – the ninth was handed over on 15 November.

September: Final Gnat public display at the Battle of Britain Days at RAF Abingdon and St Athan.

By the end of their fifteenth season the *Red Arrows* Gnats had flown 1,292 displays.

Winter: Conversion to the BAe Hawk.

15 November: The *Reds* carried out their first display with nine Hawk T1s over the BAe factory airfield at Bitteswell, Leicestershire.

1980   13 March: First public appearance with the Hawk was a display at Episkopi, Cyprus.

April: Official permission was granted for the team to have its own badge and motto 'Éclat'.

1980   6 April: The team's first UK public display flying Hawks was given at Sywell, Northants.

17 May: XX262 was written off when it hit a yacht's mast during a display off the coast at Brighton. The pilot ejected safely. It was the first *Reds* aircraft to crash in public.

1981   The *Red Arrows* Charitable Trust was established, endorsed subsequently by a policy statement from the Ministry of Defence.

1983   10 March: The team officially moved from RAF Kemble (its home since 1966) to RAF Scampton where they arrived on 5 April on return from Cyprus.

3 May: The team departed on its second North American tour, the first since it re-equipped with the Hawk.

1984   21 March: XX251 crashed at Akrotiri during spring training.

31 August: XX257 ditched in the sea off Sidmouth due to engine compressor failure.

1986   12 June: The RAF Aerobatic Team embarked on a seventeen–day Far East Tour, named *Eastern Hawk*, giving twenty-two displays in fifteen countries.

The *Red Arrows*' 2,000th display given at Bournemouth/Hurn.

⋀ The team gave their 2,000th display at Bournemouth-Hurn Airport on 1 June 1986

⋀ From April 1980 the *Red Arrows* had their own unit badge and motto 'Éclat'

⋀ Their first public display with Hawks was given in 1980 at Sywell.

⋀ There was a surprise in the *Reds'* twenty-fifth anniversary birthday cake at IAT 1989 at Fairford.

Team leader Tim Miller cutting a birthday cake to mark the *Reds'* twenty-fifth anniversary at Biggin Hill in June 1989.

1989 The twenty-fifth anniversary of the *Red Arrows* was celebrated with a display at RAF Scampton involving six aerobatic teams and was also marked with 'birthday cakes' at Biggin Hill and Fairford.

1990 The *Red Arrows* visited the Soviet Union for the first time. On their way back they gave a display in Budapest, Hungary.
15 September: The largest flypast that the team has ever participated in – the 168-aircraft Battle of Britain fiftieth anniversary flypast over Buckingham Palace and RAF Abingdon.

1991 26 August: The team formated with the RAF's Vulcan B2 bomber XH558 for the first time at the Great Warbirds Air Display at West Malling.
18–23 September: The *Reds* hosted the Sukhoi Su-27s of the Soviet Air Force *Russian Knights* at RAF Scampton for the duration of their first international appearance, which included displays at Leuchars and Finningley.

1992 September: To mark the retirement of the RAF's last Avro Vulcan, the *Red Arrows* flew in formation with XH558 at Cranfield.
September: A unique formation was flown at Bratislava, Slovakia, with a *Red Arrows* Hawk joining a *White Albatros* Aero L-39, a *Patrouille de France* Alpha Jet, *Frecce Tricolori* MB339, *Patrulla Aguila* Aviojet and Russian Test Pilot's Sukhoi Su-27.

1993 19 September: Start of the *Reds'* third North American tour. Fourteen displays were flown in the USA, together with one in Canada.

1995 23 August: The *Red Arrows'* 3,000th display was given at the official opening of the Dartmouth Royal Regatta.
October to February 1996: The team embarked on a world tour including the Middle East, South Africa, Asia (including LIMA '95 in Malaysia) and Australia.

The team in formation with the last Vulcan B2 overhead West Malling during the Great Warbirds Air Display in August 1991.

A flypast at Cranfield in September 1992 to mark the retirement of the RAF Vulcan display flight's Vulcan B2 XH558.

RAF Hercules C3 leading a *Red Arrows* flypast near Cape Town in January 1996. (Peter Mobbs)

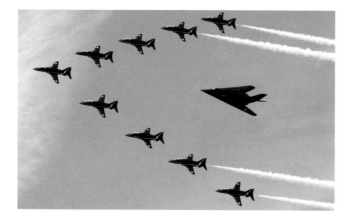

◁ RAF exchange pilot Squadron Leader Richie Matthews, a member of the *Red Arrows* 1995–97, here flying a USAF F117A Nighthawk 'stealth fighter' in formation with the Hawks at the Royal International Air Tattoo in July 2003.

1995	The team gave 136 displays, the highest number flown in any one calendar year.
1996	26 January: It is estimated that the *Reds* display was watched by its greatest ever number of spectators at Sydney on Australia Day – nearly one million people. 21 February: On its return to the UK after four months away, the team landed back at RAF Cranwell, its new home following the closure of Scampton.
1997	As part of BAe's export sales drive, the *Red Arrows* displayed at the Dubai Air Show.
2000	21 December: The *Reds* returned to RAF Scampton following a review of basing requirements.
2002	4 June: The *Red Arrows* took part in a formation flypast with a British Airways Concorde over London to mark the Queen's Golden Jubilee. August–September: The team made a short visit to Canada.
2003	July: RAF exchange pilot Sqn Ldr Richie Matthews, a member of the *Red Arrows* in 1995–97, flew a USAF F-117A Nighthawk 'stealth fighter' in formation with the team at the Royal International Air Tattoo. 25 September: Exercise *Eastern Hawk '03* began and the team undertook a five-week goodwill tour to the Middle and Far East. The tour was supported by the industry, including BAE Systems and Rolls-Royce. 17 December: The centenary of powered flight was marked by the *Reds* with a flypast over the opening of the RAF Museum Hendon's new 'Milestones of Flight' building.
2004	21 May: RAFAT's fortieth display season was officially launched.
2005	12 May: The team marked the fortieth anniversary of its first UK display with a special performance at Biggin Hill Airport.
2006	March: The team practised for two weeks at Tanagra at the invitation of the Hellenic Air Force, before flying to Cyprus for *Springhawk* 2006. Mid-May: An extensive tour included displays in Jordan, India, Oman, Abu Dhabi, Bahrain, Saudi Arabia and Greece, concluding with a major Spanish Air Force air show at San Javier on 4 June. This delayed the start of the team's UK season until 10 June.

▽ The unique sight of the *Red Arrows* flying with a Lockheed U-2 'spyplane' over Akrotiri, Cyprus in 2005.

◁ Three photographic reconnaissance Spitfires in the *Red Arrows* 'box' at RIAT 2005.

▷ Flypast over Buckingham Palace marking the Queen's 80th birthday on 17 June 2006, with the RAF's last Canberra PR9 XH134 accompanying the *Red Arrows*. *(Denis Calvert)*

▷ The fortieth anniversary of the RAF's VC10 was marked by this formation at RIAT 2006.

▷ The *Reds'* 4,000th display was given at RAF Leuchars on 9 September 2006.

△ Battle of Britain Memorial Flight: Hurricane and three Spitfires with the *Red Arrows* at Fairford during RIAT 2007.

2006 17 June: There was a flypast marking the Queen's 80th birthday over Buckingham Palace, with the RAF's last Canberra PR9 XH134 accompanying the *Red Arrows*.
9 September: The RAF Leuchars Air Show hosted the *Red Arrows'* 4,000th display.

2007 October: A slightly revised livery was unveiled, with a prominent Royal Air Force title added to the white fuselage stripe.

△ Emirates Boeing 777 flying with the Red Arrows over Dubai in 2007.

△ Virgin Atlantic Airline's twenty-fifth anniversary was commemorated at the 2009 Biggin Hill Air Fair with a flypast by the *Red Arrows* and the airline's specially painted Boeing 747 *Lady Penelope*. (Paul Fiddian)

◁ A quartet of Typhoons flew over Tower Bridge, London, on 1 April 2008 with the *Red Arrows*, marking the ninetieth anniversary of the RAF. (Denis Calvert)

▷ The *Red Arrows'* first female pilot on pre-season training in Cyprus.

2008	1 April: A quartet of Typhoons flew with the *Red Arrows* over Tower Bridge, London to mark the ninetieth anniversary of the RAF.
	20 May: The MoD announced a permanent team move to RAF Scampton. Later, this plan was revised.
	June–July: The team's *Western Arrow* North American tour included a first ever New York City display (over the Hudson River) and a flypast with a USAF F-22 Raptor in Virginia.
	5 September: A flight with the *Red Arrows* was a Help for Heroes charity auction's star lot. It was won by an unprecedented £1.5 million bid.
2009	May: Flt Lt Kirsty Moore became the first female pilot to be selected for the team.
	28 June: Virgin Atlantic Airline's twenty-fifth anniversary was commemorated at the Biggin Hill Air Fair with a special flypast involving the team and the airline's specially painted Boeing 747 *Lady Penelope*.

△ Vulcan XH558 with the *Reds* at Dawlish in August 2009, one of a number of similar post-restoration flypasts made at UK airshows. (Paul Fiddian)

2009   20 August: At the Dawlish Airshow, the *Red Arrows* and Avro Vulcan B2 XH558 – reflown in October 2007 – flew together for the first time in seventeen years.

2010   23 March: That season's *Synchro Pair* – Flt Lts Mike Ling and David Montenegro – collided in Crete while rehearsing the 'Opposition Barrel Roll'. Neither pilot was seriously injured but XX233 was written off.

2011   20 August: Flt Lt Jon Egging crashed while breaking from the formation to land at Bournemouth Airport after a beachfront display.

8 November: Flt Lt Sean Cunningham died after what is believed to have been a Hawk ejection seat and parachute failure on the ground at RAF Scampton.

2012   March: Flt Lt Kirsty Stewart (formerly Moore) left the team. To maintain the formation's symmetry *Red 8*, Flt Lt Dave Davies, was withdrawn from display duty. Except for high-profile flypasts, the team flew with seven Hawks throughout 2012.

June: The MoD announced that RAF Scampton would continue to be the *Red Arrows*' home base for at least eight more years.

26 July: Full-team flypasts were carried out over all of the London 2012 live sites, concluding with an Olympic Stadium flypast prior to the Games' Opening Ceremony.

11–12 August: The team participated in the Russian Air Force's centenary event at Zhukovsky Air Base near Moscow.

2013   February: During pre-season training the 2013 team flew the first nine-Hawk formation since 2011.

May: Saluting the WW2 US Eagle Squadron pilots, the *Red Arrows* flew with a Hurricane, Spitfire, P-47 Thunderbolt and P-51 Mustang at the IWM Duxford Spring Airshow.

△ Squadron Leader Jim Turner led a reduced team of seven Hawks through the 2012 season.

▷ The 4,500th display by the *Red Arrows* was clocked up at RAF Waddington on 6 July 2013.

△ In a salute to the Second World War US Eagle Squadron pilots, the *Red Arrows* flew with a Hurricane, Spitfire, P-47 Thunderbolt and P51 Mustang at the IWM Duxford Spring Air Show in May 2013

2013   20–21 July: British Airways' first Airbus A380 and an Airbus A400M each formated with the *Red Arrows* in flypasts unique to the Royal International Air Tattoo.

           4 November: The team left the UK for a month-long major tour of the Middle East, giving displays at the Dubai Air Show, the Aerobatic Show in Abu Dhabi, as well as Qatar, Bahrain, Oman, Kuwait and visits to Jordan and Saudi Arabia.

2014   11 July: Flypast at RIAT 2014 with aircraft from the *Patrouille de France*, *Frecce Tricolori*, *Patrouille Suisse* and *Breitling Jet Team* saluting the *Red Arrows'* 50th display season.

◁ The *Red Arrows* flew with British Airways' first Airbus A380 airliner on the first day of the RIAT 2013 at RAF Fairford. (Jamie Hunter)

▷ On the second day of RIAT 2013 the team escorted the new Airbus A400M Atlas military transport in the display.

◁ 50th display season salute at the Royal International Air Tattoo at RAF Fairford in July 2014. (Katsuhiko Tokunaga)

▽ The *Red Arrows* stole the show at the Dubai Air Show during their Middle East tour in November 2013. (Jamie Hunter)